CELEBRATIONS

By Arnold Adoff

ANTHOLOGIES

BLACK ON BLACK
Commentaries by Black Americans

BLACK OUT LOUD
An Anthology of Modern Poems by Black Americans

BROTHERS AND SISTERS
Modern Stories by Black Americans

CITY IN ALL DIRECTIONS
An Anthology of Modern Poems

I AM THE DARKER BROTHER
An Anthology of Modern Poems by Black Americans

IT IS THE POEM SINGING INTO YOUR EYES
Anthology of New Young Poets

MY BLACK ME
A Beginning Book of Black Poetry

SISTERS OF THE WORD
Anthology of New Women Poets

THE POETRY OF BLACK AMERICA
Anthology of the 20th Century

BIOGRAPHY

MALCOLM X

POETRY/PICTURE BOOKS

BIG SISTER TELLS ME THAT I'M BLACK

BLACK IS BROWN IS TAN

MAKE A CIRCLE   KEEP US IN: POEMS FOR A GOOD DAY

MA NDA LA

TORNADO! POEMS

WHERE WILD WILLIE

CELEBRATIONS
A New Anthology of Black American Poetry

COMPILED AND EDITED BY Arnold Adoff

INTRODUCED BY Quincy Troupe

FOLLETT PUBLISHING COMPANY  Chicago

Acknowledgments

Selections by the following poets are included by permission of the poet, agent and/or publisher. This list continues on p. 269 and constitutes an extension of the copyright page.

SAMUEL ALLEN (PAUL VESEY): "Nat Turner" copyright © 1972 by Samuel Allen, and reprinted with his permission.

RUSSELL ATKINS: "Inner-City Lullaby" from *Poetry Now*. Copyright © 1975 by *Poetry Now*. Reprinted by permission of Russell Atkins. "Probability and Birds" from *Here In The* by Russell Atkins (Cleveland State University Press and Poetry Center). Copyright © 1976 by Russell Atkins and reprinted with his permission. "'DANGEROUS CONDITION:' Sign on Inner-City House" reprinted by permission of Russell Atkins.

ALVIN AUBERT: "When the Wine was Gone" from *Feeling Through: New Poems by Alvin Aubert*. Copyright © 1976 by Alvin Aubert, and reprinted with his permission.

AMIRI BARAKA (LEROI JONES): "Ka 'Ba," "Young Soul," "Ballad of the Morning Streets," "Tight Rope," "Leadbelly Gives an Autograph," "Funeral Poem," "SOS," "Black People: This Is Our Destiny," and "Cold Term" from *Black Magic Poetry 1961–1967* by Amiri Baraka (LeRoi Jones) (Bobbs-Merrill Company). Copyright © 1969 by LeRoi Jones. Reprinted by permission of the publisher, The Bobbs-Merrill Company, and The Sterling Lord Agency, Inc.

GEORGE BARLOW: "Mellowness & Flight," and "Sweet Diane" from *Gabriel* by George Barlow (Broadside Press). Copyright © 1974. Reprinted by permission of Broadside Press.

(continued on page 269)

ISBN 0-695-40699-X   Titan binding
ISBN 0-695-80699-8   Trade binding

Library of Congress Catalog Card Number: 76-19888

23456789/8281807978

Dedication:

For my children, Leigh and Jaime

For their sisters and brothers
     of every race and every wonderful
          combination of races

For Charles Mingus

For the memory of Booker Ervin
     and all who stop too soon

Direction:

The words will remain and the music
     will sing in our heads

Celebrate and use the power
     and the love

Stand free and take control

Preface

IN THESE MOST DIFFICULT OF TIMES

The publication of this new anthology of Black American poetry marks my tenth anniversary as an editor and anthologist. *CELEBRATIONS* is my tenth collection of contemporary literature. My fifth anthology of Black American poetry for young people and their older friends.

This is a double celebration. It has been twenty years since I began teaching in New York City schools. Since I began collecting poetry to use with my students.

There have been many changes during that time. Changes in style and language and music. The fabric of the multiple society that is American has been stretched and changed. Here and there. The fabric of the multiple poetries that is American has been stretched and changed. Here and there. There are new fabrics. Prefabrication. Paint by numbers. Poet by numbers. Polyester poets. Drip and dry. Plastic poems.

But fine poetry, crafted and singing, has remained. And new poets continue to drive for excellence. Unique vision and unique expression of that vision are still the criteria. There is still the need to convey that vision and expression to others. The need to warn and sing and catalogue and celebrate. Poets continue to work through indifference and hostility to teach for change. The reasons remain.

And young people remain interested and involved. Youngsters who need a solid breakfast along with a solid poem. Warm houses and excellent schools and meaningful work. Youngsters who need poems that run the line from past to future. Poems that lift the head from page to sky. Lift the feet from the floor. Move the spirit from a full belly and survival struggles. Poems and people. These reasons remain.

This anthology presents 240 poems by 85 Black American poets of this century. These are some of the finest poems of several generations of a literature. There is a balance and representation of age and sex, location and style. Major poets and major work alongside newer poets and pieces. Work from published volumes together with poems from manuscript. Much work from chapbooks and publications that no longer exist. The small presses that have presented much of the production of contemporary Black poetry. The sources.

The collection has a general purpose and theme. *CELEBRATIONS* sums it up. The past and the present. The heroes and heroines. Ordinary people living lives that inspire. That create the myth and method for a people. For all people.

The poems are organized into twelve sections. Each has a theme and flow that holds the work together. The total of the sections creates a chronological and thematic unity. From "The Idea of Ancestry" and "Lineage," through "The Southern Road," "Young Soul," and "True Love." "A Poem for Heroes." "Shade." Finally, "For Each of You."

In these most difficult of times, this anthology presents the tradition and future of Black American poetry to young people of every race and background. During these times of busing and resistance to busing, of integration and equality struggles, these poems can educate for the long ride we all take together. During these times of censorship battles and liberation struggles, we can all go from these Black specifics to the human universals all poets use and present. The universals that count.

Remember the ancestors and their past and our past. Learn the lessons of that past. Sing the songs. Love the loves. Grow strong and take control of our lives and futures. Move forward together.

Arnold Adoff
Yellow Springs, Ohio
1977

Introduction

A new anthology of African-American poetry is always a welcome addition to the whole of American literature; it is also a welcome event and a definite cause for celebration. It is a welcome event because it, the poetry, has always informed African-Americans — and other Americans as well — in a much-needed spiritual and realistic way of where we Americans have been in any given time throughout our history. It has illuminated and recorded that place, almost always, with a greater clarity and insight than has any other discipline, with the possible exception of African-American music. It is a cause for celebration precisely because of the many obstacles placed in the paths of many African-American poets and their poetry by the publishing industry of this country. Getting a volume of poetry by an African-American poet published — no matter how good the poet is — almost always amounts to a small miracle.

Throughout its history, the United States has been a totally barbarous and racist place for African-Americans to live, and so it stands to reason that our poets would be accorded the very same treatment that any other Black person would receive, the so-called liberalism of the arts notwithstanding. In fact, the spoken, written, and visual arts are among the foremost bastions of racism in this country, probably ranking just below the Ku Klux Klan and the John Birch Society. Only three African-American writers have received either a National Book Award or a Pulitzer Prize for literature. Gwendolyn Brooks received the Pulitzer Prize for poetry in 1950; Ralph Ellison, the National Book Award for fiction in 1952; and Virginia Hamilton, the National Book Award for children's literature in 1975. Robert Hayden received, in 1976, the Academy of American Poets Fellowship and is presently the Consultant in Poetry to the Library of Congress, the first African-American to ever hold that prestigious post.

But of all the areas of artistic endeavor, that of poetry is probably the most racist. It seems as though, for the most part, White American poets — whether they be young or old, male or female, traditionalist or classicist, and even those who consider themselves to be avant-garde — still remain hostile to the idea of accepting a Black person as a poet. And their odious, obsequious advance people, publicists and advertising personnel, editors, and those who front and pass themselves off as critics and academicians have refused, in most instances, to either acknowledge critically or deal fairly with — in their classrooms as well as in their "high-brow" literary journals and magazines — the overwhelmingly and obviously great oeuvre that is African-American poetry. But then again, we — African-Americans and other Americans who do understand — can hardly expect people to deal fairly with something the greatness and grandeur of which they do not have the wherewithal to either appreciate or understand, though many of them sometimes seem to recognize the power and unbelievable beauty that shines from the best of African-American poetry. This power and beauty is especially apparent when that poetry is presented in its oral form, which, in my opinion, is always the best way to present any poetry. Perhaps many White American poets and critics are intimidated — in the same way that many White musicians were intimidated by Black musicians — by the power, impassioned rhythms, fresh and original uses of language and form, and the metaphoric beauty — extended or otherwise — and brilliance that characterizes the best of our poetry. Poets and poetry are the guardians of the language of any nation, and in the United States, African-American poets are and have been some of this nation's most vigilant sentinels.

In this century African-American poets, starting with Paul Laurence Dunbar, have written some of the most original and penetrating poetry that this country has produced. Such poets as Jean Toomer, Claude McKay, Countee Cullen, Langston Hughes, Sterling A. Brown, Melvin B. Tolson, Owen Dodson, Robert Hayden, Margaret Walker, Gwendolyn Brooks, Dudley Randall, and Lance Jeffers, among a host of older and very good poets, have carved out places for themselves equal to those of any poets writing in this country during the first half of this century. And some of the contributions of Langston Hughes, Jean Toomer, Sterling A. Brown, Melvin B. Tolson, Robert Hayden, Gwendolyn Brooks, Owen Dodson, and Margaret Walker rank among the greatest achievements in poetry anywhere in the world during this century.

But it remains for the youngest poet mentioned above, Lance Jeffers, to serve as a bridge between the two older generations — those poets of the Harlem Renaissance period and those of the "post"-renaissance decades of the 30s, 40s, and 50s — and the generation of poets who emerged during the 1960s and 70s. Jeffers, who was born in 1919, has been generally overlooked, but he is a very important "bridge" figure to many young poets who saw in his work a likeness to their own. Jeffers, in both his older and recent work, anticipated and conveyed more clearly than anyone else of his generation the raw rage that was to flow like a lava river of fire from the great apocalyptic flowering of poetry that burst upon the literary scene during the 1960s. This anticipation is evident in the language Jeffers uses in many of his poems. It is a kind of tortured language of rage, a sort of rage that seems to be trying to break through the walls of oppression, and it is a rage that sometimes turns in on itself, seemingly out of frustration, as in the lines "and my own dark rage a rusty knife with teeth to gnaw/my bowels."[1] The anticipation is also there — and a reechoing of the Harlem Renaissance motif — in the cosmic idea of hope and idealism, as in the lines "My blackness is the beauty of this land."[2]

The above two lines quoted from Jeffers illustrate two im-

[1] Lance Jeffers, "My Blackness Is the Beauty of This Land" from *My Blackness Is the Beauty of This Land* (Detroit: Broadside Press, 1970).
[2] Ibid.

port'ant themes that recur time and time again throughout African-American poetry written during the 1960s. These two themes, the rage turning in on itself at the same time that it is lashing out, and the cosmic idea of hope and idealism (transformed in the 60s into the motif of self-awareness complete with the notion of self-beauty as being a universal and superior beauty) anticipate the tortured early poetry of Amiri Baraka (at that time LeRoi Jones), as in his line "I am inside someone who hates me."[3] The self-glorification of the Jeffers line "My blackness is the beauty of this land" is continued in the 60s in the work of Baraka, Sonia Sanchez, Haki R. Madhubuti, and Askia Touré, among others.

But if these two themes dominated much of the published poetry of the 1960s, and they did, they were only "the tip of the iceberg." For after the Black Arts Movement poetry of that combustible era, the strength and genius of the subsequent work of the late 1960s and the 1970s was in the many different poetic voices and styles — in the diversity, like a brilliant rainbow, to which the period gave rise. This diversity, though hard fought for (there were and still are many casualties from the many "ideological" battles), has in turn bred a greater depth and richness in the poetry being written today by African-American poets.

Poetry at its best has always been a reflection of the society from which it springs. And the best poets have many times prophesied and chronicled more perceptively than have historians, the social and political climate and the cultural mores of any given time and place. Thus the poets of the Harlem Renaissance period reflect the spirit of the beginnings of a collective consciousness among African-Americans of that period, just as the poets of the early and mid-1960s reflect that period of flaming revolt, Black Power slogans, and FBI-ordered murders. But the poets of the 60s also extended and built upon the precedents established by Langston Hughes, James Weldon Johnson, and Sterling A. Brown of returning to African-Ameri-

---

[3]"As Agony, As Now" from *The Dead Lecturer* (New York: Grove Press, 1964).

can roots and folklore, and of using the folk forms and their rhythms, such as the blues, spirituals, ballads, work songs, and jazz, in a fusionistic way in their own poetry.

The mid-to-late 1960s saw the largest African-American audience for poetry. Hundreds and even thousands of African-American people (witness the historic "Black Spirits" readings that took place in New York City in 1971 at the Apollo Theater and the Brooklyn Academy of Music) crowded into theaters, coffeehouses, parks, churches, community centers, classrooms, and lecture halls to listen and to be moved by young poets reading poetry that brilliantly reflected and articulated the concerns of the masses of African-American people. It was phenomenal. Overnight, young poets became as famous as many recording, film, and athletic stars. For the first time in our history, poetry—pulling the rest of our literature with it—came to and occupied center stage. Poets became political and social spokespersons—which most already were in their poetry. Then the fights and hassles began. Names were called. Everyone began to argue over just what a poem—especially a *Black* poem—actually was. Was it didactic or personal? Were all White people bad and none good? Longtime friendships broke up over certain uses of metaphor, and even over whether metaphor was, in fact, "ideologically" plausible to the Black struggle in the first place. Everyone began to have a theory on just what poetry was supposed to do. Everybody's theory was different. Confusion reigned. Poets split up into camps. There was the so-called Watts school of poetry, the Chicago school, the New York school, the Cleveland school, the New Orleans school, and the Detroit school, and inside these "schools" there were other schools. Poets began to sharpen up their words and load their poems with bullets. They started aiming their poems at poets whom they had known and respected for years. Stupid poetic wars began. Casualties mounted. Many poets, when they realized what was happening, packed up their words and deserted. Others, who saw and understood what was happening from the beginning, never entered the fracas. Others escaped and were lost in the bedeviling, electronic skies of addicting mass media. Many disappeared completely, never to be heard from again.

But however tragic and frustrating the era of the 1960s actually was, the gains made during the period were profoundly significant. Publishing houses were established. Broadside Press, under the direction and editorship of Dudley Randall, began publishing, and many outstanding poets, among them Sonia Sanchez, Haki R. Madhubuti, Nikki Giovanni, Doughtry Long, Judy Simmons, Etheridge Knight, and the venerable veterans Margaret Walker and Gwendolyn Brooks, had their poetry published through Broadside. Black River Writers, under the direction of Eugene Redmond, came into existence; Third World Press, led by Haki R. Madhubuti, published books of poetry by Carolyn Rodgers, Amiri Baraka, and Dudley Randall; Jihad Press under the leadership of Amiri Baraka, also began publishing. And these are just a few from a long list who began publishing in the late 60s. Reed, Cannon, and Johnson, under the joint leadership of Ishmael Reed, Steve Cannon, and Joe Johnson, began publishing in the early 70s, and their list includes such writers as Victor Hernandez Cruz, Calvin Herton, and Alison Mills. Magazines and journals have also flourished over the last decade. Strictly literary publications such as *Black World* (now *First World*), *Confrontation: A Journal of Third World Literature, Yardbird Reader, Bopp, Black Creations, Black Books Bulletin, Umbra, Hoodoo,* and *Ascensions* provided new as well as established African-American poets and writers with a much-needed platform, and were—and are—invaluable in the continuing development of our literary voices. The period also saw the beginning of such popular slick magazines as *Essence, Encore, Players,* and others. And although there were and still are questions about the aesthetics of these magazines, there is little doubt that these magazines—along with television shows like "Soul" and "Black Journal"—helped African-American writers reach a much wider audience.

The decade of the 1960s was many things to many people. It was a beautiful, uplifting, inspiring, and magical time and era; it was also unbelievably tragic, stupid, vain, hedonistic, self-defeating, and ultimately frustrating. For a time during the early 70s the arguments begun in the 1960s prevented many of the younger writers from achieving their full potential, perhaps because of not wanting to offend one of their teachers or perhaps because of an argument that that teacher might have had with a writer the young student writer secretly admired. But that time has passed and the air has cleared, even though some traces of resentment linger on. And although some of the younger writers have been lost as a result of those unfortunate disagreements, many have survived and have pressed on to forge and write an even greater, deeper, and far more wide—ranging poetry. Although the massive crowds have dispersed, a large audience—articulate, responsive, and discriminating—still remains and is growing again.

Today there is a host of excellent young (and by young I mean under 45 years of age) African-American poets who are writing better than they have ever written in their lives. Among the outstanding poets composing today are Jayne Cortez, Primus St. John, Frank Lamont Phillips, Judy Simmons, K. Curtis Lyle, Etheridge Knight, Lucille Clifton, Michael A. Harper, June Jordan, Ishmael Reed, Calvin C. Hernton, Amiri Baraka, Haki R. Madhubuti, Carolyn M. Rodgers, Eugene Redmond, Audre Lorde, Al Young, Joyce Carol Thomas, Gerald W. Barrax, Sonia Sanchez, Bob Kaufman, Yvonne, Sam Cornish, Ntozake Shange, Norman Jordan, George Barlow, Carole Gregory Clemmons, Stanley Crouch, Alvin Aubert, Nikki Giovanni, Charles Lynch, Ron Welburn, Horace Coleman, Tom Weatherly, Joe Johnson, Conyus, Doughtry Long, Amus Mor, David Henderson, Elouise Loftin, Sterling Plumpp, and the legendary Watts poet, Ojenke (Alvin Saxon). The poets mentioned above are writing some of the most vigorous, imaginative, and powerful poetry anywhere in the world today.

And so it is with a sense of celebration that we turn to this new anthology of African-American poetry. Celebration because the world is alive—however desperate the straits we are in—and because the state of African-American poetry is healthy in 1977. In any anthology there will always be costly and sometimes unavoidable omissions, and this anthology is no different in that respect. One could have wished for fewer poems from one poet and more from another. Or on the other hand one could have wished to see more of one's own favorite poems. But this is a personal thing, and any anthology reflects the personal choices and biases of its editor — and that, I think, is as it should be. This is a strong anthology, however, and the strength of the collection — as in almost every anthology of which Arnold Adoff has been the editor — lies in the diversity of the poets chosen and in the various voices by which Adoff has chosen to represent them. All good poets write in more than one voice, and in choosing, in most instances, more than one poem to represent a poet, Adoff has given us a chance to hear those "other" voices.

Yes, the state of African-American poetry in 1977 is healthy, and if the indications that I see around me every day are signs of what is to come, it will probably get healthier as we head into the 1980s. For this we are thankful and encouraged. The current year has witnessed the tremendous impact of Alex Haley's important saga, *Roots,* and I am convinced that some of the poets in this collection will extend that impact, will add to it. And so we celebrate Arnold Adoff's *Celebrations,* celebrate the distinctly different voices that make up the fabric of this anthology. For in the end it is important that *all* the different voices be heard because African-Americans have always spoken in more than one voice, no matter what some of the self-serving special interest groups would have us believe. The voices of African-American poetry are as varied as those of African-American music. Which poets of the younger group will become the most important? Only "time will tell," as Malcolm X has reminded us. Indeed it will. Doesn't it always?

The important thing is to read these poets. Rise and fall, be joyous and sad with them. Allow yourself to journey inside their world of words and rhythms. Listen to their rhythms, let the words inform your eyes. These are significant poets for significant times. And if you listen and read them closely enough and allow them to come into your heart and mind, perhaps what they are saying to you will cause you to look at the world in a different light, will perhaps take you to a new and illuminated level of consciousness. And if this happens — and I feel certain that it will — we will all be better because of it. For as Ted Joans, that special, globe-trotting, African-American troubadour-poet has reminded us: "you have nothing to fear from the poet but the truth."

Quincy Troupe
New York
1977

The Idea of Ancestry

Africa

LUCILLE CLIFTON

home
oh
home
the soul of your
variety
all of my bones
remember

from: African Poems

HAKI R. MADHUBUTI (DON L. LEE)

WE'RE an Africanpeople
hard-softness burning black.
the earth's magic color our veins.
an Africanpeople are we;
burning blacker softly, softer.

from: Beginnings

ROBERT HAYDEN

I
Plowdens, Finns,
Sheffeys, Haydens,
Westerfields.

Pennsylvania gothic,
Kentucky homespun,
Virginia baroque.

        II
A shotgun on his shoulder,
his woman big with child and
shrieking curses after him,

Joe Finn came down from
Allegheny wilderness
to join Abe Lincoln's men.

Goddamning it survives the
slaughter at the Crater.
Disappears into his name.

        III
Greatgrandma Easter, on my father's side,
was a Virginia freedman's Indian bride.
She was more than six feet tall. At ninety could
still chop and tote firewood.

Runagate Runagate

ROBERT HAYDEN

I.

Runs falls rises stumbles on from darkness into darkness
and the darkness thicketed with shapes of terror
and the hunters pursuing and the hounds pursuing
and the night cold and the night long and the river
to cross and the jack-muh-lanterns beckoning beckoning

and blackness ahead and when shall I reach that
        somewhere
morning and keep on going and never turn back and
        keep on going.

        Runagate
                Runagate
                        Runagate

Many thousands rise and go
many thousands crossing over

                        O mythic North
                O star-shaped yonder Bible city

Some go weeping and some rejoicing
some in coffins and some in carriages
some in silks and some in shackles

        Rise and go fare you well

No more auction block for me
no more driver's lash for me

    If you see my Pompey, 30 yrs of age,
    new breeches, plain stockings, negro shoes;
    if you see my Anna, likely young mulatto
    branded E on the right cheek, R on the left,
    catch them if you can and notify subscriber.
    Catch them if you can, but it won't be easy.
    They'll dart underground when you try to catch them,
    plunge into quicksand, whirlpools, mazes,
    turn into scorpions when you try to catch them.

And before I'll be a slave
I'll be buried in my grave

    North star and bonanza gold
    I'm bound for the freedom, freedom-bound
    and oh Susyanna don't you cry for me

        Runagate
                Runagate

II.

Rises from their anguish and their power,

       Harriet Tubman,

       woman of earth, whipscarred,
       a summoning, a shining

       Mean to be free

And this was the way of it, brethren brethren,
way we journeyed from Can't to Can.
Moon so bright and no place to hide,
the cry up and the patterollers riding,
hound dogs belling in bladed air.
And fear starts a-murbling, Never make it,
we'll never make it. *Hush that now,*
and she's turned upon us, leveled pistol
glinting in the moonlight:
Dead folks can't jaybird-talk, she says;
you keep on going now or die, she says.

Wanted Harriet Tubman   alias The General
alias Moses   Stealer of Slaves

In league with Garrison   Alcott   Emerson
Garrett   Douglass   Thoreau   John Brown

Armed and known to be Dangerous

Wanted   Reward   Dead or Alive

Tell me, Ezekiel, oh tell me do you see
mailed Jehovah coming to deliver me?

Hoot-owl calling in the ghosted air,
five times calling to the hants in the air.
Shadow of a face in the scary leaves,
shadow of a voice in the talking leaves:

Come ride-a my train

Oh that train, ghost-story train
through swamp and savanna movering movering,
over trestles of dew, through caves of the wish,
Midnight Special on a saber track movering movering
first stop Mercy and the last Hallelujah.

Come ride-a my train

Mean mean mean to be free.

Frederick Douglass
ROBERT HAYDEN

When it is finally ours, this freedom, this liberty, this beautiful
and terrible thing, needful to man as air,
usable as earth; when it belongs at last to all,
when it is truly instinct, brain matter, diastole, systole,
reflex action; when it is finally won; when it is more
than the gaudy mumbo jumbo of politicians:
this man, this Douglass, this former slave, this Negro
beaten to his knees, exiled, visioning a world
where none is lonely, none hunted, alien,
this man, superb in love and logic, this man
shall be remembered. Oh, not with statues' rhetoric,
not with legends and poems and wreaths of bronze alone,
but with the lives grown out of his life, the lives
fleshing his dream of the beautiful, needful thing.

from: Stars

ROBERT HAYDEN

III
(Sojourner Truth)

Comes walking barefoot
out of slavery

ancestress
childless mother

following the stars
her mind a star

Crispus Attucks

ROBERT HAYDEN

Name in a footnote. Faceless name.
Moot hero shrouded in Betsy Ross
and Garvey flags — propped up
by bayonets, forever falling.

Nat Turner

SAMUEL ALLEN (PAUL VESEY)

From the obscurity of the past, we saw
the dark now flaming face of a giant Nathaniel
calling
whosoever will
let him come.

Turner's face softened for a moment
and he mourned for the lost years
 the eternity of grief
 the thousands, the millions of his people
 torn from the soil of their fathers
 for a living death in a strange land.

And his face hardened
and we heard, again, the voice, calling
 whosoever will
 let him come
 let him come, now
 let him come
 let him come
 let him come.

Memorial Wreath

For the more than 200,000 Negroes who served
in the Union Army during the Civil War

DUDLEY RANDALL

In this green month when resurrected flowers,
Like laughing children ignorant of death,
Brighten the couch of those who wake no more,
Love and remembrance blossom in our hearts
For you who bore the extreme sharp pang for us,
And bought our freedom with your lives.

         And now,
Honoring your memory, with love we bring
These fiery roses, white-hot cotton flowers
And violets bluer than cool northern skies
You dreamed of in the burning prison fields
When liberty was only a faint north star,

Not a bright flower planted by your hands
Reaching up hardy nourished with your blood.

Fit gravefellows you are for Lincoln, Brown
And Douglass and Toussaint . . . all whose rapt eyes
Fashioned a new world in this wilderness.

American earth is richer for your bones;
Our hearts beat prouder for the blood we inherit.

Ancestors

DUDLEY RANDALL

Why are our ancestors
always kings or princes
and never the common people?

Was the Old Country a democracy
where every man was a king?
Or did the slavecatchers
take only the aristocracy
and leave the fieldhands
laborers
streetcleaners
garbage collectors
dishwashers
cooks
and maids
behind?

My own ancestor
(research reveals)
was a swineherd
who tended the pigs
in the Royal Pigstye

and slept in the mud
among the hogs.

Yet I'm as proud of him
as of any king or prince
dreamed up in fantasies
of bygone glory.

Strong Men

The strong men keep coming on.
                    —Sandburg

STERLING A. BROWN

They dragged you from the homeland,
They chained you in coffles,
They huddled you spoon-fashion in filthy hatches,
They sold you to give a few gentlemen ease.

They broke you in like oxen,
They scourged you,
They branded you,
They made your women breeders,
They swelled your numbers with bastards . . . . .
They taught you the religion they disgraced.
You sang:

      Keep a-inchin' along
      Lak a po' inch worm . . .

You sang:

      By and bye
      I'm gonna lay down this heaby load . . .
You sang:

      Walk togedder, chillen,
      Dontcha git weary . . .
          The strong men keep a-comin' on
          The strong men get stronger.

They point with pride to the roads you built for them,
They ride in comfort over the rails you laid for them.
They put hammers in your hands
And said—Drive so much before sundown.
You sang:
> Ain't no hammah
> In dis lan'
> Strikes lak mine, bebby,
> Strikes lak mine.

They cooped you in their kitchens,
They penned you in their factories,
They gave you the jobs that they were too good for,
They tried to guarantee happiness to themselves
By shunting dirt and misery to you.
You sang:
> Me an' muh baby gonna shine, shine
> Me an' muh baby gonna shine.
> > The strong men keep a-comin' on
> > The strong men git stronger . . .

They bought off some of your leaders
You stumbled, as blind men will . . .
They coaxed you, unwontedly soft-voiced . . .
You followed a way.
Then laughed as usual.
They heard the laugh and wondered;
Uncomfortable;
Unadmitting a deeper terror . . .
> > The strong men keep a-comin' on
> > Gittin' stronger . . .

What, from the slums
Where they have hemmed you,
What, from the tiny huts
They could not keep from you—
What reaches them
Making them ill at ease, fearful?
Today they shout prohibition at you

"Thou shalt not this"
"Thou shalt not that"
"Reserved for whites only"
You laugh.

One thing they cannot prohibit—

> The strong men . . . coming on
> The strong men gittin' stronger.
> Strong men . . .
> Stronger . . .

An Old Woman Remembers

STERLING A. BROWN

Her eyes were gentle; her voice was for soft singing
In the stiff-backed pew, or on the porch when evening
Comes slowly over Atlanta. But she remembered.

She said: "After they cleaned out the saloons and the dives
The drunks and the loafers, they thought that they had better
Clean out the rest of us. And it was awful.
They snatched men off of street-cars, beat up women.
Some of our men fought back, and killed too. Still
It wasn't their habit. And then the orders came
For the milishy, and the mob went home,
And dressed up in their soldiers' uniforms,
And rushed back shooting just as wild as ever.
Some leaders told us to keep faith in the law,
In the governor; some did not keep that faith,
Some never had it: he was white too, and the time
Was near election, and the rebs were mad.
He wasn't stopping hornets with his head bare.
The white folks at the big houses, some of them
Kept all their servants home under protection

But that was all the trouble they could stand.
And some were put out when their cooks and yard-boys
Were thrown from cars and beaten, and came late or not at all.
And the police they helped the mob, and the milishy
They helped the police. And it got worse and worse.

"They broke into groceries, drug-stores, barber shops,
It made no difference whether white or black.
They beat a lame bootblack until he died,
They cut an old man open with jack-knives
The newspapers named us black brutes and mad dogs,
So they used a gun butt on the president
Of our seminary where a lot of folks
Had sat up praying prayers the whole night through.

"And then," she said, "our folks got sick and tired
Of being chased and beaten and shot down.
All of a sudden, one day, they all got sick and tired.
The servants they put down their mops and pans,
And brooms and hoes and rakes and coachman whips,
Bad niggers stopped their drinking Dago red,
Good Negroes figured they had prayed enough,
All came back home — they'd been too long away —
A lot of visitors had been looking for them.

"They sat on their front stoops and in their yards,
Not talking much, but ready; their welcome ready:
Their shotguns oiled and loaded on their knees.

"And then
There wasn't any riot any more."

Strange Legacies

STERLING A. BROWN

One thing you left with us, Jack Johnson.
One thing before they got you.

You used to stand there like a man,
Taking punishment
With a golden, spacious grin;
Confident.
Inviting big Jim Jeffries, who was boring in:
"Heah ah is, big boy; yuh sees whah Ise at.
Come on in. . . ."

Thanks, Jack, for that.

John Henry, with your hammer;
John Henry, with your steel driver's pride,
You taught us that a man could go down like a man,
Sticking to your hammer till you died.
Sticking to your hammer till you died.

Brother,
When, beneath the burning sun
The sweat poured down and the breath came thick,
And the loaded hammer swung like a ton
And the heart grew sick;
You had what we need now, John Henry.
Help us get it.

So if we go down
Have to go down

We go like you, brother,
'Nachal' men. . . .

Old nameless couple in Red River Bottom,
Who have seen floods gutting out your best loam,
And the boll weevil chase you
Out of your hard-earned home,

Have seen the drought parch your green fields,
And the cholera stretch your porkers out dead;
Have seen year after year
The commissary always a little in the lead;
Even you said
That which we need
Now in our time of fear, —
Routed your own deep misery and dread,
Muttering, beneath an unfriendly sky,
"Guess we'll give it one mo' try.
Guess we'll give it one mo' try."

Black Star Line

HENRY DUMAS

My black mothers I hear them singing.

Sons, my sons,
dip into this river with your ebony cups.
A vessel of knowledge sails under power.
Study stars as well as currents.
Dip into this river with your ebony cups.

My black fathers I hear them chanting.

My sons, my sons,
let ebony strike the blow that launches the ship!
Send cargoes and warriors back to sea.
Remember the pirates and their chains of nails.
Let ebony strike the blow that launches this ship!
Make your heads not idle sails, blown about
by any icy wind like a torn page from a book.

Bones of my bones,
all you golden-black children of the sun,

lift up! and read the sky
written in the tongue of your ancestors.
It is yours, claim it.
Make no idle sails, my sons.
Make heavy-boned ships
to bring back sagas from Melle, Songhay, Kongo,
deeds and words of Malik, Marcus, Toussaint,
and statues of Mahdi.
Make no idle ships of pleasure.
Remember the pirates.
For it is the sea who owns the pirates,
not the pirates the sea.

My black mothers I hear them singing.

    Children of my flesh,
dip into this river with your ebony cups.
A ship of knowledge sails unto wisdom.
Study what mars and what lifts up.
Dip into this river with your ebony cups.

Generations

JUDY DOTHARD SIMMONS

1863, my great grandmother —
    cut eleven years from Cherokee cord
    reared to wait upon her half-relations
    a servant in the kitchen of her father —

drank of freedom from a rusty pail
    by the dirt-floored shanty where her mother,
    wife now to an African transplanted,
    conceived and bore the black half of our kin

ate meal gruel with a scraped hog jowl that
    man and woman earned in dawn-dusk labor

planting, hoeing, picking for her father
cyclicly creating cotton snow

spurred the gathered pine knots' daylight burning
lest the night be met without salute
rose and slept and rose from corn-husk pallets
to feed the fire, starve the morning chill

1953, my silent mother
rode a slat-bed truck to dusty fields
knelt on brown sky picking cotton clouds
brought home three dollars earned in dawn-dusk labor

I carried water, chopped dead pine
grateful that the summer used no coal
played, I guess, and had the supper waiting:
atonement for her wheeze and swollen hands

in winter she taught school for croppers' wages
breathed coarse smoke and soot from coal-stoked stoves
soothed and scolded fifty first-grade children
heard her rich contralto rasp, kept on

1970, and I, the daughter —
cut these ninety years from Cherokee cord
reared for twenty-six in proper manner
fit, at last, to join my father's mainstream —

live in corporate rooms with blanched relations
find most still a crasser kind of father
hear them talk as through a one-way window
the speech of self-reflection, stupid, blind

feel the killing fury of four lifetimes
explode through coal gas tunnels in my eyes
but cap the pits with poems, so stay alive
to carry on tradition:
                    we survive

The Old People Speak of Death
QUINCY TROUPE

the old people speak of death
frequently now
my grandmother talks of those now
gone too spirit
now less than bone

they speak of shadows
that graced their days with darkness
or either light speak of days & corpses
of relationships buried deeper
then residue of bone
gone now beyond hardness
gone now beyond form

they sing from ingrown roots
of beginnings those who have left us
& climbed through the holes we left in our eyes
for them too enter through

eye walk back now
through holes eye left in my eyes
for them too enter through too where
eye see them now darker than where roots begin
lighter than where they go
with their spirits
heavier then stone

& green branches will grow
from these roots darker than time
blacker than the ashes of nations
& wave in sun-tongued mornings
shadow the spirits in our eyes

they have gone now
with their spirits too fuse

with greenness enter stone & glue
their invisible faces
upon the transmigration of earth
nailing winds & sing their guitar
voices through the ribcages
of our days
darker than where roots begin
greener than what they bring

the old people speak of death
frequently now
my grandmother talks of those now
gone too spirit
now less than bone

Daybreak

FRANK LAMONT PHILLIPS

By that withering oak
of night and its bird passing
overhead in the moonlight, merely
a shadow, the waters of the
Mississippi ride their mud base into
infinity. Now the water, soft
in what light there is, swallows
the moon with its mouth before daybreak.

In my mother's house, in
my half sleep and far from my
day in the factory heat, I
am near her love, once tight as a fist,
and her age and sickness, now
the only hands she holds as held
mine in weak embrace before sleep.

And Spring green and wood
smooth into cement and city lights
that turn on with the dark, ending
only at daybreak when they with
a sigh, cease. St. Louis on the bank,
at the dock of the steamships, waits
like a beau for the River Queen.

In the house, in the gold cage
of dining room worn velure, her
fond canary chirping the night
air is all the beau she knows. Maurice
sings the River Queen's song, and
I've seen her dance the old
dances with abandon and belief in
                                yesterday.

She is aged now. I am the
last good love, that one remained. In
my imagination we dance
on the deck of the Admiral, the
chandalier's cascading light
about our heads. Are able

then to see the night in silences
as lovers paused from their
brief interlude. Smiling.

In the darkness the sky upon
itself in waves. The canary
singing to himself in his cage
is swallowed by the dark before dawn.

The Dark Way Home: Survivors

MICHAEL S. HARPER

Married to rural goldmines
in southern Minnesota,
your money is land, horses,
cows all of metal:
the area is German;
the religion Gothic, acute,
permanent, in white heat
and telephone wires;
you live with a family where
each issue is food,
where word is appetite
you hunger in: hunting
your slough for teal;
beating your sons with machinery
and your oiled might;
setting your chickens to peck
your children; roping them homegrown
to the tractors and cuckleburs,
giving them no private thoughts
but rebellion:
fish and hunt for surplus
acreage to corncrib you up,
lutheran or catholic
in taste and ambition;
love grandchildren,
love potatoes,
love beans, love venison,
love pheasant, love berries,
love bass, love rocks
become fossils, love sweetcorn,
shucked in guts, silently
burrowing what grows
but can't love, burgeoning,
lovely, like this.

Breath in My Nostrils

LANCE JEFFERS

Breath in my nostrils this breasty spring day
shouts a jubilee
like one of my old sweaty fathers
in the surge of song and
sweetness of green trees and
the steamy blacky earth,
he lifted his head to a wildhorse tilt
and forgot that he was a slave!

The Idea of Ancestry

ETHERIDGE KNIGHT

1

Taped to the wall of my cell are 47 pictures: 47 black
faces: my father, mother, grandmothers (1 dead), grand
fathers (both dead), brothers, sisters, uncles, aunts,
cousins (1st & 2nd), nieces, and nephews. They stare
across the space at me sprawling on my bunk. I know
their dark eyes, they know mine. I know their style,
they know mine. I am all of them, they are all of me;
they are farmers, I am a thief, I am me, they are thee.

I have at one time or another been in love with my mother,
1 grandmother, 2 sisters, 2 aunts (1 went to the asylum),
and 5 cousins. I am now in love with a 7 yr old niece
(she sends me letters written in large block print, and
her picture is the only one that smiles at me).

I have the same name as 1 grandfather, 3 cousins, 3 nephews,
and 1 uncle. The uncle disappeared when he was 15, just took
off and caught a freight (they say). He's discussed each year
when the family has a reunion, he causes uneasiness in
the clan, he is an empty space. My father's mother, who is 93
and who keeps the Family Bible with everybody's birth dates
(and death dates) in it, always mentions him. There is no
place in her Bible for "whereabouts unknown."

2

Each Fall the graves of my grandfathers call me, the brown
hills and red gullies of mississippi send out their electric
messages, galvanizing my genes. Last yr/like a salmon quitting
the cold ocean — leaping and bucking up his birthstream/I
hitchhiked my way from L.A. with 16 caps in my pocket and a
monkey on my back. and I almost kicked it with the kinfolks.
I walked barefooted in my grandmother's backyard/I
        smelled the old
land and the woods/I sipped cornwhiskey from fruit jars
        with the men/
 I flirted with the women/I had a ball till the caps ran out
 and my habit came down. That night I looked at my
        grandmother
and split/my guts were screaming for junk/but I was almost
contented/I had almost caught up with me.
(The next day in Memphis I cracked a croaker's crib for a fix.)

This yr there is a gray stone wall damming my stream, and
        when
the falling leaves stir my genes, I pace my cell or flop on
        my bunk
and stare at 47 black faces across the space. I am all of them,
they are all of me, I am me, they are thee, and I have no sons
to float in the space between.

Lineage

Lineage

MARGARET WALKER

My grandmothers were strong.
They followed plows and bent to toil.
They moved through fields sowing seed.
They touched earth and grain grew.
They were full of sturdiness and singing.
My grandmothers were strong.

My grandmothers are full of memories
Smelling of soap and onions and wet clay
With veins rolling roughly over quick hands
They have many clean words to say.
My grandmothers were strong.
Why am I not as they?

now poem.   for us.

SONIA SANCHEZ

don't let them die out
all these old / blk / people
don't let them cop out
with their memories
of slavery / survival.
                    it is our
heritage.
          u know. part / african.
part / negro.
              part / slave
sit down with em brothas & sistuhs.
                         talk to em. listen to their

tales of victories / woes / sorrows.

                                    listen to their blk /

myths.

          record them talken their ago talk

for our tomorrows.

                       ask them bout the songs of

births. the herbs

              that cured

                     their aches.   the crazy /

                             niggers blowen

                             some cracker's cool.

the laughter

comen out of tears.

let them tell us of their juju years

          so ours will be that much stronger.

The Old Women Still Sing
For Alice Walker and Arthenia J. Bates Millican

CHARLES H. ROWELL

The old women, like the oaks and the red clay of that land,
      strong and solid,
Can be heard in the late of afternoon, standing over hot
      stoves
Making supper of ham hocks and greens or just fatback and
      bread
For their men returning with plows from fields or bottles
      from joints;
Or sitting in rockers or porches with funeral parlor fans in
      hand,
Singing songs their mothers sang, songs their mothers'
      mothers sang—
Not songs of wars and victories, nor songs of kings and
      queens in regalness,

But songs of hope and love, songs of praise and thanks,
        songs of troubles and joy.

The old women of my land can be heard
Singing their lives, yours and mine.

#4

DOUGHTRY LONG

Where my grandmother lived
there was always sweet potato pie
and thirds on green beans and
songs and words of how we'd
survived it all.
Blackness.
And the wind
a soft lull
in the pecan tree
whispered
Ethiopia
        Ethiopia, Ethiopia
E-th-io-piaaaaa!

Jesus Drum

PEARL CLEAGE LOMAX

her hand that holds
this drum
is brown and wrinkled
like a withered peach.
clutching and beating

in a rhythm I know.
the hand that strikes
this drum
i have touched
or had touch me
in times when Sundays
were a day of singing
and Grandmothers talked in circles
of love
and Jesus fell like silver
from their mouths.

Oya

AUDRE LORDE

God of my father discovered at midnight
my mother asleep on her thunders
my father
returning at midnight
out of tightening circles of anger
out of days' punishment
the inelegant safety of power
Now midnight empties your house of bravado
and passion sleeps like a mist
outside desire
your strength splits like a melon
dropped on our prisoners floor
midnight glows
like a jeweled love
at the core of the broken fruit.

My mother is sleeping.
Hymns of dream lie like bullets
in her nights weapons

the sacred steeples
of nightmare are secret and hidden
in the disguise of fallen altars
I too shall learn how to conquer yes
Yes yes god
damned
I love you
now free me
quickly
before I destroy us.

A Grandfather Poem

WILLIAM J. HARRIS

A grandfather poem
must use words of great dignity.

It can not
contain words like:
Ubangi
rolling pin
popsicle,

but words like:
Supreme Court
graceful
wise.

Those Winter Sundays

ROBERT HAYDEN

Sundays too my father got up early
and put his clothes on in the blueblack cold,
then with cracked hands that ached
from labor in the weekday weather made
banked fires blaze. No one ever thanked him.

I'd wake and hear the cold splintering, breaking.
When the rooms were warm, he'd call,
and slowly I would rise and dress,
fearing the chronic angers of that house,

Speaking indifferently to him,
who had driven out the cold
and polished my good shoes as well.
What did I know, what did I know
of love's austere and lonely offices?

Love from My Father

CAROLE GREGORY CLEMMONS

Left like water in glasses overnight
in a cold house,
iced children are fierce.
They see fathers slobbering, staggering
into the living room chair
and race through his pockets for nickels and quarters.
The cold gives the children pneumonia and sends
red balloons tied to hospital beds, and
a caseworker to turn the heat on.

There are many gifts,
other drunks sleep in thrown paper
and green wine bottles behind billboards
but my father brings fresh glazed donuts in a white bag.

Mothers

NIKKI GIOVANNI

the last time i was home
to see my mother we kissed
exchanged pleasantries
and unpleasantries pulled a warm
comforting silence around
us and read separate books

i remember the first time
i consciously saw her
we were living in a three room
apartment on burns avenue

mommy always sat in the dark
i don't know how i knew that but she did

that night i stumbled into the kitchen
maybe because i've always been
a night person or perhaps because i had wet
the bed
she was sitting on a chair
the room was bathed in moonlight diffused through
those thousands of panes landlords who rented
to people with children were prone to put in windows

she may have been smoking but maybe not
her hair was three-quarters her height
which made me a strong believer in the samson myth
and very black

i'm sure i just hung there by the door
i remember thinking: what a beautiful lady

she was very deliberately waiting
perhaps for my father to come home
from his night job or maybe for a dream
that had promised to come by
"come here" she said "i'll teach you
a poem: *i see the moon*

>   *the moon sees me*
>   *god bless the moon*
>   *and god bless me"*

i taught it to my son
who recited it for her
just to say we must learn
to bear the pleasures
as we have borne the pains

        [10 mar 72]

Big momma

HAKI R. MADHUBUTI (DON L. LEE)

finally retired   pensionless
from cleaning somebody else's house
she remained home to clean
the one she didn't own.
in her kitchen where we often talked
the *chicago tribune* served as a tablecloth
for the two cups of tomato soup that went
along with my weekly visit & talking to.

she was in a seriously-funny mood
& from the get-go she was down, realdown:

roaches around here are like
letters on a newspaper
or
u gonta be a writer, hunh
when u gone write me some writen
or
the way niggers act around here
if talk cd kill we'd all be dead.

she's somewhat confused about all this *blackness*
but said that it's good when Negroes start putting themselves
first and added: we've always shopped at the colored stores,
                 & the way niggers cut each other up round
                 here every weekend that whiteman don't
                     haveta
                 worry bout no revolution specially when
                     he's
                 gonta haveta pay for it too, anyhow all he's
                 gotta do is drop a truck load of *dope* out
                     there
                 on 43rd st. & all the niggers & yr
                     revolutionaries
                 be too busy getten high & then they'll turn
                     round
                 and fight each other over who got the
                     mostest.

we finished our soup and i moved to excuse myself.
as we walked to the front door she made a last comment:
         now *luther* i knows you done changed a lots but if
         you can think back, we never did eat too much pork
         round here anyways, it was bad for the belly.
i shared her smile and agreed.

touching the snow lightly i headed for 43rd st.
at the corner i saw a brother crying   while
trying to hold up a lamp post,
thru his watery eyes i cd see big momma's words.

at sixty-eight
she moves freely, is often right
and when there is food
eats   joyously with her own
real teeth.

Your Mother

SAM CORNISH

your mother
in the market
place searches
for fish
pinches oranges
watches prices
change for
the weekend
she checks the dirt
under the butcher's
fingernail her feet
slip in water
and fish scales
hamburger looks
dead behind dirty
counter glass
flies
even in the winter
live here

Sam's World

SAM CORNISH

sam's mother has
grey combed hair

she will never touch
it with a hot iron

she leaves it
the way the lord
intended

she wears it proudly
a black and grey
round head of hair

colors for mama

BARBARA MAHONE

when you show me
that those colors carry
special meaning in your head
i understand. there is
a sickness not your own
that makes it so. each
time you start your colortalk
you speak for me. you speak
for all of us. sanity
is colorblind.

sugarfields

BARBARA MAHONE

treetalk and windsong are
the language of my mother
her music does not leave me.

let me taste again the cane
the syrup of the earth
sugarfields were once my home.

i would lie down in the fields
and never get up again
(treetalk and windsong
are the language of my mother
sugarfields are my home)

the leaves go on whispering secrets
as the wind blows a tune in the grass
my mother's voice is in the fields
this music cannot leave me.

I Know a Lady

JOYCE CAROL THOMAS

I know a lady
A careful queen
She bows to no one
Her will is a
Fine thread of steel

Her blessing is a
Smile
Sinking its sails
Inside

Youth followed her around
The day she reached forty
Very few people knew
Her face said twenty-two

Now somebody's embroidered silver
In her hair and sketched
A wrinkle here and there

I know a lady
A careful queen
She bows to no one

for muh' dear

CAROLYN M. RODGERS

    today Blackness
  lay backin
& rootin
    told my sweet mama
     to leave me alone
     about my wild free knotty and nappy
      hair
    cause i was gon lay back
     and let it grow so high
      it could reroute its roots
      and highjack the sky!

    she sd. why don't you let it grow
     right on down to the ground honey chile,
    grow yo'self a coat of hair fuh winter
     matter fact you so BLACK now, huh!
      why don't you jest throw
      a fit
    of BLACK lay backin & rootin.

my mama gives some boss advice . . .
    i think we all ought to do that

for sapphires
For mama and daddy

CAROLYN M. RODGERS

my daddy don't know
the same lady
i do. i know mama
he knows "suga."
            and when daddy looks at mama
            i wonder does he see
            the wrinkles around
            the tight mouth, stiff
            factory used fingers
            uh yellow skin,
            begun to fade. . . .

and when mama talks
how does he hear? i hear
anger, pride, strength and love
crouched low in the throat,
any, ready to spring.
            but daddy calls mama "suga"
            and uh beacon is behind his eyes,
            he buys Chanel and coats
            with fur collars. . . .

i wonder what lady does daddy know?

Miss Rosie

LUCILLE CLIFTON

When I watch you
wrapped up like garbage
sitting, surrounded by the smell
of too old potato peels
or
when I watch you
in your old man's shoes
with the little toe cut out
sitting, waiting for your mind
like next week's grocery
I say
when I watch you
you wet brown bag of a woman
who used to be the best looking gal in Georgia
used to be called the Georgia Rose
I stand up
through your destruction
I stand up

For deLawd

LUCILLE CLIFTON

people say they have a hard time
understanding how I
go on about my business
playing my Ray Charles
hollering at the kids —
seem like my Afro

cut off in some old image
would show I got a long memory
and I come from a line
of black and going on women
who got used to making it through murdered sons
and who grief kept on pushing
who fried chicken
ironed
swept off the back steps
who grief kept
for their still alive sons
for their sons coming
for their sons gone
just pushing

Good Times

LUCILLE CLIFTON

My Daddy has paid the rent
and the insurance man is gone
and the lights is back on
and my uncle Brud has hit
for one dollar straight
and they is good times
good times
good times

My Mama has made bread
and Grampaw has come
and everybody is drunk
and dancing in the kitchen
and singing in the kitchen
oh these is good times

good times
good times

oh children think about the
good times

The Southern Road

Sun Song

LANGSTON HUGHES

Sun and softness,
Sun and the beaten hardness of the earth,
Sun and the song of all the sun-stars
Gathered together —
Dark ones of Africa,
I bring you my songs
To sing on the Georgia roads.

Daybreak in Alabama

LANGSTON HUGHES

When I get to be a composer
I'm gonna write me some music about
Daybreak in Alabama
And I'm gonna put the purtiest songs in it
Rising out of the ground like a swamp mist
And falling out of heaven like soft dew.
I'm gonna put some tall tall trees in it
And the scent of pine needles
And the smell of red clay after rain
And long red necks
And poppy colored faces
And big brown arms
And the field daisy eyes
Of black and white black white black people
And I'm gonna put white hands
And black hands and brown and yellow hands

And red clay earth hands in it
Touching everybody with kind fingers
And touching each other natural as dew
In that dawn of music when I
Get to be a composer
And write about daybreak
In Alabama.

Alabama

JUDY DOTHARD SIMMONS

back in back of the back country
after the nameless mountains —
pinestabbed and springbled —
safely beyond the county seat, Centre,
almost to Georgia and eastern
standard time (whole other dimension:
the warp of New England freedom),

the clay dessicated red roads crinkle out like
bleached ribbons
stretched in dusty green drawers of sweetgum stands,
hackberry trees, knotty white bark thin-scarred with old rust
from the clouds (by some vehicles some time gone by)
raised lonesomely, settled — like countries — the same;

pay out cross stark broken-stalked fields, the farmers
and pathcutters being, it seems,
some primeval race slipped the
clutch of mortality, leaving red trails
for a hearse

i remember how she sang

ROB PENNY

i remember how she sang
sang the blues
on east street
in opelika bama

we left
with our mother
and came to pittsburgh
to our father

blues, oh, how she sang
down in opelika

we dug socials, the turbans,
frankie lymon, the dells,
lavern baker, the el venos

east street, my, how she
could sing those blues

we learned how to snort,
to smoke reefer, to sloe
dance ("Oh, What A Night")
to play, to be slick,
to be catholics

blues, in red earth, how
she sang, gaddamn

and we never got to korea
nor to vietnam

we snort on blackness now
digs cats like malcolm leroi
jones trane stevie wonders
rob williams and sister
betty shabazz

she still sings the blues
and they go to the moon

we are evolutionary lawmakers
and punishers

down home she steady singing
those gaddamn blues
on east street
in opelika bama

1968

Mississippi Born
For Ayanna Pearl Williams

PEARL CLEAGE LOMAX

your voice sister
tells me another child has come.
your tired voice tells more
than your words or eyes will say.
sister another child has come.
and the birthroom
filled with blood and small groans
and your daughter's round eyes leaning to watch
her tiny sister born.

driving the Mississippi death roads to find you.
the childfilled jeep bumps and jiggles
until i cannot tell if the riding or the fear
thrusts my heart into my throat.
emmett till fills my head like damp cottom
and chaney's neshoba nightmare is more real
on this road that slithers toward Meridian,
Jackson, Sunflower County, Braxton and D'Lo.

your house squatting in the midst of clots
of dry dirt crumbled for the futile planting.
and crouched in the dark cave of that room
you greeting me. tired
and sick of being sick here.
wild eyes gleaming in wild face and the lump
of mewing new one curled like a sleeping slug beside you.

am i real to you now?
remember the night of your first leaving?
your long blue scarf doublewrapped against the cold
at the end of that week when we could not laugh
together without collapsing into giggles and tears
laying our watery cheeks against the cool dry bathroom
        porcelin
hugging each other and hugging ourselves.

are you real to me now?
swishing away the constant flies and rocking the new one
and thinking that the flies whisper of death and decay
and cannot be allowed to skitter across her tiny red face.
sister sister.
another child has come.

The Song Turning Back into Itself 3

AL YOUNG

Ocean Springs Missippy
you dont know about that
unless youve died in magnolia
tripped across the Gulf
& come alive again
or fallen in the ocean
lapping up light
like the sun digging

into the scruffy palm leaves
fanning the almighty trains
huffing it choo-choo
straight up our street
morning noon & nighttrain
squalling that moan
like a big ass blues man
smoking up the sunset

Consider the little house
of sunken wood
in the dusty street
where my father would
cut his fingers
up to his ankles
in fragrant coils
of lumber shavings
the backyard of nowhere
Consider Nazis & crackers
on the same stage
splitting the bill

Affix it all to
my memory of Ma
& her love of bananas
the light flashing
in & out of our lives
lived 25¢ at a time
when pecans were in season
or the crab & shrimp
was plentiful enough
for the fishermen
to give away for gumbo
for a soft hullo
if you as a woman
had the sun in your voice
the wind over your shoulder
blowing the right way
at just that moment in history

Knoxville, Tennessee

NIKKI GIOVANNI

I always like summer
best
you can eat fresh corn
from daddy's garden
and okra
and greens
and cabbage
and lots of
barbecue
and buttermilk
and homemade ice cream
at the church picnic
and listen to
gospel music
outside
at the church
homecoming
and go to the mountains with
your grandmother
and go barefooted
and be warm
all the time
not only when you go to bed
and sleep

Church Poem

JOYCE CAROL THOMAS

The smell of sage
Mingles with burnt hair
And mama prepares Sunday dinner
On Saturday night
Chicken and dressing
Whisper promises
In the ear you hold
    with one hand
So your edges will be straight
As she does your hair

"Bend your head so you
    won't get burnt"
If you bend your head
on Saturday evening
Is it the same God
You bend to on Sunday morning?

Mama, how long do you
    beat the cake
Until your arms get too sore
    to beat some more
But Betty Crocker says 4 minutes
This ain' no white folks cake
    I aim to bake

Now line up with lye soap
and bath towel, pajamas,
Slippers and robes
Sink into the hot tin tub
Scrub off a week's worth
    of dirt
Grease down in cold cream
And warm your backside
By bubbling fire

On the Sabbath morning
The organ begins its descent
Choir comes rocking
Down the aisle
Like so many black notes
Stroking the carpet floor
And rising til rested by
Elsa's wanded finger
Sister Elsa's First Sunday
Sermon in song
Holding a phrase
Kneading it like new dough
Turning it round
     in her head
Singing it different
       everytime
You can hear her shout
"Take me to the water"
Then adding in a whisper
"I know I got religion"
"I been baptized"

Did you feel the water
Riding over your feet
Sucking up the white garment
Kissing the breath
From your mouth
When she moaned
"I been baptized"

I saw a silent man leap
Straight up in the air
Sit down, then go striding
Across the room
To sit again
Understanding
The Disciplined Notes

in Undisciplined song
The unofficial concert

When does the melody end
And where does it begin?
YPWW, BYU, Bible Drill
In shiny legs
and velvet ribbons

Testimony service
And Brother Jackson shouted
Then danced the pewed benches
Front row to back
Because I held my breath
He never missed a step

It is the same God
You bend to now on Sunday morning
When does the melody end
And where does it begin?

Roll Call: A Land of Old Folk and Children

ISAAC J. BLACK

I walk downhill, slow,
        to the shanties. There,
I sing Georgia, Georgia —
        my suit, like armor to me,
a hooray and hallelujah
        to them, the townsfolk
(they're barefoot, you see)

I'm from New York, I say,
        Leroy's son-in-law.

And it's like going home:
    Mali, Kenya, Africa
as my eyes, to the rhythm
    play their faces
the sun, and the earth too . . .

But it's a strange roll call
    as I marvel there
looking for their young folk,
    who, no future here
(June mimics
her missing son)
my camera cannot shoot.

Talking to the Townsfolk in Ideal, Georgia
(June 1974)

ISAAC J. BLACK

The bones of our fathers
    old stoneface says
lie buried here:
    do rot, shrivel, to ash.

They lie, sadly he says,
    deeper than your years
but not deeper, no,
    than the blood that sank.

In Mississippi they smile too.
    And if you dig, he says,
you won't find the bones,
    the blood, but the bullets.

Home

SAM CORNISH

home
where my
ground
is

my children
born

my mother's
bone

against the
black

of dirt

the weight
of my father's

box

Southern Mansion

ARNA BONTEMPS

Poplars are standing there still as death
And ghosts of dead men
Meet their ladies walking
Two by two beneath the shade
And standing on the marble steps.

There is a sound of music echoing
Through the open door
And in the field there is
Another sound tinkling in the cotton:
Chains of bondmen dragging on the ground.

The years go back with an iron clank,
A hand is on the gate,
A dry leaf trembles on the wall.
Ghosts are walking.
They have broken roses down
And poplars stand there still as death.

sometimes i think of maryland . . .

JODI BRAXTON

big old houses have passed away
like summer's dust

green apples/polk salad/the A.M.E. Church
blue sky and Rev. Baddy's sermon
the safety of grandma's rocker
a lullaby from her knee/her sweet voice
her hands so clean and praying/or scolding
she tends her mother's grave
her father was a slave

"go to sleepy little baby
go to sleepy little baby
when you wake patty patty cake
ride a big white pony"

a brown flood breaks the banks
down at the branch/where i wrote my first poem
and flowers bloom in a vacant yard
where there was once a house/with a porch
and six low steps with carpet painted on

i place my head next to earth
and listen deep for voices
recognition/memory
song

close my hand over empty soil
where once grew corn and collards
and tomatoes 2 lbs. big

close my eyes to see the patchwork quilt
of time and impossibility
that covers me like kente cloth
and i close my eyes to see
no longer growing up but older
a woman who bleeds with the moon
and waits for a child
to burden with this heritage.

Untitled

LUCILLE CLIFTON

i went to the valley
but i didn't go to stay

i stand on my father's ground
not breaking.
it holds me up
like a hand my father pushes.
Virginia.

i am in Virginia,
the magic word
rocked in my father's box
like heaven.
the magic line in my hand.   but
where is the Afrika in this?

except the grass is green,
is greener he would say.
and the sky opens a better blue
and in the historical museum
where the slaves
are still hidden away like knives
I find a paper with a name i know.
his name.
their name.
Sayles.
the name he loved.

i stand on my father's ground
not breaking.
there is an Afrikan in this
and whose ever name it has been
the blood is mine.

my soul got happy
and i stayed all day

For Edwin R. Embree

OWEN DODSON

In countries where no birds are alive
Time bleeds into dreams children have
Of green sweet days of spring,
Of lollypops and kites.

In towns where all the shadows
Are in different places and the seasons
Of our thoughts have changed, killing
Whatever bloomed before in freedom and love,
Men hug blighted night:
Night covers their own damage:
They dream with torn blankets over their heads.

In a cabin where her sons are represented
By gold stars,
A black mother hears the present circumstance
In Tennessee or Georgia,
Sits in her rocking chair
And cracks her knuckles while she prays.

Time bleeds, shadows shift, knuckles crack.
Winter cancels spring, summer and fall.
Despair rises first thing every morning
And goes about his business
Ringing doorbells, calling: Howdy-do!

What we answer is our salvation or our end:
Some cry: I've been expecting you,
                    the coffee's on the stove.
                    The children are washing
                    behind their ears.
                    Take a seat; sit down.

They are lost before the first shine of the new sun.

Time bleeds, shadows shift, knuckles crack—
But there is a time of healing coming
When shadows will shift to normal,
A time of bright birds

And children without blood spotting their dreams:
Because there are still men whose hearts
Bear the large optimistic burden of freedom and peace:
Men who rise up early
And labor through the day for other men.

Time bleeds, shadows shift
But there is a time of healing coming
Because these men of strength are with us.

The Southern Road

DUDLEY RANDALL

There the black river, boundary to hell,
And here the iron bridge, the ancient car,
And grim conductor, who with surly yell
Forbids white soldiers where the black ones are.
And I re-live the enforced avatar
Of desperate journey to a savage abode
Made by my sires before another war;
And I set forth upon the southern road.

To a land where shadowed songs like flowers swell
And where the earth is scarlet as a scar
Friezed by the bleeding lash that fell (O fell)
Upon my fathers' flesh. O far, far, far
And deep my blood has drenched it. None can bar
My birthright to the loveliness bestowed
Upon this country haughty as a star.
And I set forth upon the southern road.

This darkness and these mountains loom a spell
Of peak-roofed town where yearning steeples soar
And the holy holy chanting of a bell
Shakes human incense on the throbbing air
Where bonfires blaze and quivering bodies char.
Whose is the hair that crisped, and fiercely glowed?
I know it; and my entrails melt like tar
And I set forth upon the southern road.

O fertile hillsides where my fathers are,
From which my griefs like troubled streams have flowed,
I have to love you, though they sweep me far.
And I set forth upon the southern road.

Where Is the Black Community?

.

Where Is the Black Community?

JOYCE CAROL THOMAS

Where is the Black community?
holding down the corner
where 3rd street meets B

sitting in the second pew
at Double Rock Baptist Church

Where is the Black community?
at Bob's Barber Shop
busting jokes about the man

at the Delta sisters
fashioning J. Magnin and new hairdos

Where is the Black community?
Scrubbing chitlin grease
off a kitchen stove eye

and hawking Muhammad Speaks
on a Stanford campus

Where is the Black community?
transplanting kidneys
in a university hospital

and plowing cotton
in a Mississippi dawn

Where is the Black community?
teaching English
at Duke and Purdue

and arranging 4 kids
in a twin sized bed

Where is the Black community?
living in two story houses
on Poplar Street Drive

and swilling Old Crow
out of a crystal flask.

in the inner city
LUCILLE CLIFTON

in the inner city
or
like we call it
home
we think a lot about uptown
and the silent nights
and the houses straight as
dead men
and the pastel lights
and we hang on to our no place
happy to be alive
and in the inner city
or
like we call it
home

Harlem in January
JULIA FIELDS

There at the top of the world
Frozen like a star
All winter long
Whose silent nightmare
Are you now

Whose theme for headlines
For legislation or reform?
The sun's asleep.
The streets are quiet.
Like a ghost you hover.
And who cares that tomorrow
You will arise like spectres,
Like thunder make a sound
Stacatto, roar from an uneasy
moment, vanish.
There at the top of the
Indifferent world
Frozen like a star
All winter long you are.

The Still Voice of Harlem

CONRAD KENT RIVERS

Come to me broken dreams and all
     bring me the glory of fruitless souls,
I shall find a place for them in my gardens.

Weep not for the golden sun of California,
     think not of the fertile soil of Alabama . . .
nor your father's eyes, your mother's body
     twisted by the washing board.

I am the hope of your unborn,
     truly, when there is no more of me . . .
there shall be no more of you. . . .

"DANGEROUS CONDITION:"
Sign on Inner-City House
RUSSELL ATKINS

From such old boards
shack'd for a fall,
infatuated with fire,
hallways too dark
for quest, hood-like
with hollow about
thick as a spell—
roam with a cruel grasp
"dangerous condition,"
whammy of eyes

      what follow-up?
seek out the lives
with a rifle
for a bulldozer?

to the death?

Inner-City Lullaby
RUSSELL ATKINS

Enough of a day has come to pass:
trashbags are on the treelawn
by the hydrant (trashbags
that have to be thick bound
because of the stray dogs
gnashing for food)

The thermostat's turned down low
because the wind might overstir—
send the furnace to too high
a pressure—the red hand
and the black hand
over far too far for an old house.
I've checked the gas range,
the screen door is latched fully
and the house door firmly fixed,
the key drawn from the lock
                    and put aside
The side door's latched and clasped,
clasped the bathroom window
I have drawn the back pantry curtains
and the cat, contrary to being put out,
is brought in
                    and fed for sleep

Detroit City

JILL WITHERSPOON BOYER

thieves give more to blue
than hardness does
and where noon is
thirty floors of steel won't tell
now that time ticks
instead of filling spaces
and tenderness talks fast

thieves give more to dusk
than engines do
and what neon offers stars
makes beggars laugh

while birds stand by without applauding
the strangeness in the songs
that asphalt sings to trees

Pigeon

I'm gon move up to the country and paint my mailbox blue.
—Taj Mahal

ELOUISE LOFTIN

Do any thing anything you will
But dont run
Love can be so beauty full and
Love can be so uguly
Ever made birds fly away
Early in the mornin when you just comin home
When the park just gets light and you aint
Nothin but a big foot steppin in wonderin
Who you belong to lookin all night for somebody
You love to take the world in you and make it right
Do anything any thing you will
But dont run
Love can be so beauty full and
Love can be so uguly
Dear God
On my one good knee
Early in the mornin
All the birds up'd and up'd away from me
And I got to purge this B-52 nightmare comin down
And dont nobody want this crazy love of mine
And I dont want to believe something's wrong with me
Cause the city is a monster and the mountains crackin up
And Nixon is elected again as usual and like it or not
Said the lady on the train with a smile on her face

There's still some hope for some good ole integration
And mama suckin her teeth and everybody lookin at me
With they hand stuck out but don't nobody want this crazy
        love I got
And the ladies goin crazy cause the men is too
And the line broke with my last pair of everthing included
        my nerves
And I'm standin here too short to reach just yet studyin this
        pole
And I got some more ands when these run out monster city
        blues
And the late night fm man wants to give me the news mind
        you
And I'm rollin pennies all night between my knees and
        starvation
Do you think that before I leave for the country
Do anything any thing you will
And I hear bird
But dont run
I wont just think pigeon

A Trip on the Staten Island Ferry

AUDRE LORDE

Dear Jonno
there are pigeons who nest
on the Staten Island Ferry
and raise their young
between the moving decks
and never touch
ashore.

Every voyage is a journey.

Cherish this city
left you by default
include it in your daydreams

there are still
secrets
in the streets
even I have not discovered
who knows
if the old men
who shine shoes on the Staten Island Ferry
carry their world
in a box slung across their shoulders
if they share their lunch
with birds
flying back and forth
upon an endless journey
if they ever find their way
back home.

One Year to Life on the Grand Central Shuttle

AUDRE LORDE

If we hate the rush hour subways
who ride them every day
why hasn't there been a New York City Subway Riot
some bloody rush-hour revolution
where a snarl
goes on from push to a shove
that does not stop
at the platform's edge
the whining of automated trains
will drown out the screams
of our bloody and releasing testament
to a last chance or hope of change.

But hope is counter-revolutionary.
Pressure cooks
but we have not exploded
flowing in and out instead each day
like a half-digested mass
for a final stake impales our dreams
and watering down each trip's fury
is the someday foolish hope
that at the next stop
some door will open for us
to fresh air and light and home.

When we realize how
much of us is spent
in rush hour subways
underground
no real exit
it will matter less
what token we pay
for change.

A Birthday Memorial to Seventh Street

AUDRE LORDE

I.

I tarry in days shaped like the high staired street
where I became a woman
between two funeral parlors next door to each other
sharing a dwarf
who kept watch for the hearses
Fox's Bar on the corner
playing happy birthday to a boogie beat
Old slavic men cough in the spring thaw
hawking

painted candles cupcakes fresh eggs
from under their dull green knitted caps
when the right winds blow
the smell of bird seed and malt
from the breweries across the river
stops even our worst hungers.

One crosstown bus each year
carries silence into overcrowded hallways
plucking madmen out of the mailboxes
from under stairwells
from cavorting over rooftops in the full moon
cutting short the mournful songs that used to soothe me
before they would cascade to laughter every afternoon
at four PM
behind a door that never opened
Then masked men in white coats dismount
to take the names of anyone
who has not paid the rent in three months
they peel off layers of christmas seals
and batter down the doors into bare apartments
where they duly note the shape of each obscenity
upon the wall
and hunt those tenants down
to make new vacancies.

II.

These were some of my lovers who were processed
through the corridors of Bellevue Mattewean Brooklyn State
the Women's House of D. St. Vincent's and the Tombs
to be stapled on tickets for a one way ride
on the unmarked train that travels
once a year
across the country east to west
filled with New York's rejected lovers
ones who played with all their stakes
who could not win nor learn to lie—
we were much fewer then—

who failed the entry tasks of Seventh Street
and were returned back home
to towns with names like Oblong and Vienna
(called Vyanna)
Cairo Sesser Cave-In-Rock and Legend.
Once a year the train stops unannounced .
at midnight
just outside of town
returning the brave of Bonegap and Tuskegee
of Pawnee Falls and Rabbittown
of Anazine and Elegant and Intercourse
leaving them beyond the edge of town
like dried up bones sucked clean of marrow
but rattling with city-like hardness
the soft wood
petrified to stone in Seventh Street.
The train screams
warning the town of coming trouble
then moves on.

III.

I walk over Seventh Street
stone at midnight
two years away from forty
and the ghosts of old friends
precede me down the street in welcome
bopping in and out of doorways
with a boogie beat
Freddie sails before me like a made-up bat
his Zorro cape just level with the stoops
he pirouettes over the garbage cans
a bundle of drugged delusions   .
hanging from his belt
while Joan with a hand across her throat
sings
unafraid of silence anymore
and Marion who lived on the scraps of breath

left in the refuse of strangers
searches the gutter with her nightmare eyes
tripping over the brown girl
young in her eyes and fortune
nimble as birch
and I try to recall her name
as Clement comes
smiling from a distance
his finger raised in counsel
or in blessing
over us all.

Seventh Street swells into midnight
memory ripe as a bursting grape
my head is a museum
full of other people's eyes
like stones in a dark churchyard
where I kneel praying
that my children
will not die politely
either.

Samurai and Hustlers

JOE JOHNSON

Horn and Hardart is closing.
We wait behind chipped cups,
We are old men in long coats.
    in the rain
We are the cadre of rude owls with violet tongues,
    in the rain
our skin is a progression of numbers,
    in the rain

black is the color of movement
black is the absence of color
        in the rain
silence explodes and a swollen dog on water waits,
        in the rain
time repeats fire
        in the rain
we are samurai and hustlers
        in the rain

And Was Not Improved

LERONE BENNETT

Let them keep it
whatever it is
for white only hides.
And smiles.
I was in the pale inn
after the writs
after the whores
after the hilariously lonely
convention men
and was not improved
and wondered why
anyone bothered.
I was in the mausoleum
with the corpses
and counted the bones
and was sad.
I went up high
and came down
and hurried home
to you

and hugged the broken-glass ghetto
and was glad
and wondered again
why anyone bothered.

April 68

SAM CORNISH

somewhere cities burn
my wife is sleeping
i touch her face
and find the cheeks
are wet
there is something
being said

Man Thinking About Woman

HAKI R. MADHUBUTI (DON L. LEE)

some thing is lost in me,
like
the way you lose old thoughts   that
somehow seemed unlost at the right time.

i've not known it or you many days;
we met as friends with an absence of strangeness.
it was the month
that my lines got longer & my metaphors softer.

it was the week   after
i felt the city's narrow breezes rush about
me
looking for a place to disappear
as   i walked the clearway,
sure footed in used sandals screaming to be replaced

your empty shoes (except for used stockings)
partially hidden beneath the dresser
looked at me,
as i sat thoughtlessly   waiting
for your touch.

that day,
as your body rested upon my chest
i saw the shadow of the
window blinds   beam
across the unpainted ceiling
going somewhere
like the somewhere i was going
when
the clearness of yr/teeth,
& the scars on yr/legs stopped me.

your beauty: un-noticed by regular eyes   is
like   a blackbird resting
on a telephone wire   that moves
quietly with the wind.

a southwind.

At Long Last

LINDSAY PATTERSON

I saw you walking
On Fifth Avenue,

Threading thru the crowd,
Aloof. Head held unusually high for a native
An ocean away,
Thinking perhaps of
Those balmy days
In Gabon.
At first you rebuffed
My glances, in favor of the fairer races.
But now I could go and throw
My arms around you
On Fifth Avenue,
Oblivious to the roar of the
Crowd. We, two, alone.
I in my red velvet dashki
That everyone says looks
So good on me,
And you in your tan corduroy
Gayla that makes you stand out
Even in a festive crowd.

New and Old Gospel

NATE MACKEY

       The pillows wet our faces with
the sweat of soft
leaves. And ragmen pick
the city like
sores. The gummed
hush of watered
    grasses fondles our
unrest, and as
outside the approach
of autumn whispers all our

unkept secrets
         random winds unkink what hints your
hair lets fall. And
bits of rainbow wet the
floor and voices
punish what was silence.
As stars walk the
         backs of our
heads our heads
turn waking,
         while
         we press for what at last
will be our lives
to be so,
         soon.

Ka 'Ba

AMIRI BARAKA (LEROI JONES)

A closed window looks down
on a dirty courtyard, and black people
call across or scream across or walk across
defying physics in the stream of their will

Our world is full of sound
Our world is more lovely than anyone's
tho we suffer, and kill each other
and sometimes fail to walk the air

We are beautiful people
with african imaginations
full of masks and dances and swelling chants
with african eyes, and noses, and arms,

though we sprawl in grey chains in a place
full of winters, when what we want is sun.

We have been captured,
brothers. And we labor
to make our getaway, into
the ancient image, into a new

correspondence with ourselves
and our black family. We need magic
now we need the spells, to raise up
return, destroy, and create. What will be

the sacred words?

Young Soul

Young Soul

AMIRI BARAKA (LEROI JONES)

First, feel, then feel, then
read, or read, then feel, then
fall, or stand, where you
already are. Think
of your self, and the other
selves . . . think
of your parents, your mothers
and sisters, your bentslick
father, then feel, or
fall, on your knees
if nothing else will move you,

           then read
           and look deeply
           into all matters
           come close to you
           city boys—
           country men

           Make some muscle
           in your head, but
           use the muscle
           in yr heart

Boys. Black.
a preachment

GWENDOLYN BROOKS

Boys. Black. Black Boys.
Be brave to battle for your breath and bread.

Your heads hold clocks that strike the new time of day.
Your hearts are
legislating Summer Weather now.
   Cancel Winter.

Up, boys. Boys black. Black boys.
Invade now where you can or can't prevail.
Take this:
   there's fertile ground beneath the pseudo-ice.
Take this:
   sharpen your hatchets. Force into the green.
Boys, in all your Turnings and your Churnings,
remember Afrika.
Call your singing and your bringing,
your pulse, your ultimate booming in
the not-so-narrow temples of your Power —
call all that, that is your Poem, AFRIKA.
Although you know
so little of that long leaplanguid land,
our tiny union
is the dwarfmagnificent.
Is the busysimple thing.

See, say, salvage.
Legislate.
Enact our inward law.

In the precincts of a nightmare all contrary
be with your sisters hope for our enhancement.
Hurry.
Force through the sludge.
Wild thick scenery subdue.
Because
the eyeless Leaders flutter, tilt, and fail.
The followers falter, peculiar, eyeless too.
Force through the sludge. Force, whether
God is a Thorough and a There,
or a mad child,

playing
with a floorful of toys,
mashing
whatwhen he wills. Force, whether
God is spent pulse, capricious, or a yet-to-come.

And boys,
young brothers, young brothers —
beware the imitation coronations.
Beware
the courteous paper of kingly compliments.

Beware
the easy griefs.
It is too easy to cry "ATTICA"
and shock thy street,
and purse thy mouth,
and go home to thy "Gunsmoke." Boys,
black boys,
Beware the easy griefs
that fool and fuel nothing.

I tell you
I love You
and I trust You.
Take my Faith.
Make of my Faith an engine.
Make of my Faith
a Black Star. I am Beckoning.

A Grandson Is a Hoticeberg

MARGARET DANNER

A grandson is
not
the wing-sprouting cherub
that I, as a doting grandmother
have persisted in seeing and showing.

A grandson is a
      hot
         ice
            berg,
that one cannot retain or disdain,
with all the half submerged knowing grinnings,
lusty leerings and/or jeerings
that the name implies.

And as an added distraction or attraction
(according to ones politics)
this grandson is a
      BLACK
         hot
           ice
              berg,
with bushy head hung down
and lengthy legs sprawled up
over the easiest-to-dirty chair.

And stubby fingernails thrown out in
"V for victory"
and grubby fists thrust to the polluted air
in cries of
"POWER TO THE PEOPLE . . . FIGHT"
and King Kong combs rearing up out of his
"this is an AFRO . . . MAN" hair.
And orangegreengoldblue
SHIKIS

and ebony with ivory eyed
TIKIS
and rather than the
"Yes mam, grandmother"
that he had been taught;
a jolting of "aints . . . wonts"
and other igniting Black language revolts,
and defyings of
        "RIGHT ON
                MOTHERS
                        MOTHER,
      DYNAMITE . . ."

Love Necessitates

EUGENE REDMOND

Grandmother's love
Was sometimes her wrath:
      Quick caresses with switch or ironing cord.

My young unhoned hide knew
Volcanic
Voodoo
Vengeance:
Sting-swift payment for unperformed errands and orders;
Rod and wrath for tarrying too long under Black Bridge.

One did not sass Grandma,
Whose love was stern and firm:
Precise preparation (mercy!)
For the Academy of Hard Knocks.

Sweet Diane
For Diane Ramirez

GEORGE BARLOW

I see that you're a poetry lover, sweet Diane,
little Fifth Grade diamond girl,
lonely little student of mine.
You say that you don't like P.E.,
that you'd rather "make poems" —
me too, baby, me too.

So we sit here on a frozen December bench,
make frosty conversation,
and watch a crucial kickball game.
It's cold out here —
too cold for these little *chilums*.

You say your best friend was offed?
A teen-age boy cracked her head
with a big rock? (Damn!)
And she died in Brookside Hospital on Halloween?
Did this really happen,
or is it the glitter
of your sweet Fifth Grade imagination?

Wish I could believe you made it up.
But I can't.
It's real, baby,
too real for all of us.

What did you do with your tears?
Did you make a poem, sweet Diane?
All this cold, that big rock,
And your dead girlfriend
are the reflections of our world.
Why don't you shine back on them
with a poem this afternoon?
Why don't you save us
with a poem, sweet Diane?

Deborah Lee

YVONNE

I am ten and no one I love has died.
My copper penny loafers
crush the brownest leaves.
My legs are quick, oiled,
and straight as finished wood.
My socks are more red than Mackintosh apples.
They are beating like home-coming
wings under my skirt.
My skirt, a great and pleated maple leaf.
My arms, angora cardinal's wings.
They are carrying David Copperfield,
an unfinished Deerslayer.
They are carrying a hard New England apple.

It is Saturday. I travel heavy
with benevolence and approval.
I am my mother's education.
I am my grandmother's heart.
The grandfathers nod and smile, the invalids
hire me to polish their nails.
I may rummage through their charity
jewelry. I may listen
to the wages of Negro day's work.
I am never jostled at the cartoon matinee.
I do not roller skate in jeans at the Olympian.
I am trading my David Copperfield
for Great Expectations.
Miss Mundy has a starched face, but takes
my child's card without question.

I do not want to be a nun.
Inside my pocket are crystal rosary beads.
They are my diamonds.
Inside Dickens is a gold-edge Murillo.

It is my bookmark.
I will pin my mind to long Chinese dresses.
I will do something for my people.
I wear no scapular.
I will double my sins in confession.
"Once I studied bel canto,"
old Sister Saint Philomena
remarked now
almost gospel contralto.
God, I will not be a nun.

God, I would not steal from anybody.
My mother is dying in her life.
My grandmother's hands are claws.
The polish cannot hide the ammonia burns.
God, I want to do something for my people.
Mother bought my skirt
with the sale of two out-grown winter coats.
My shoes will last from September
to September. I do not
roller skate. I do not want
to be jostled.
I am not stealing from anybody.

Emma

YVONNE

It was Mama who was partial
to Aunt Viney, my father's sister.
It was Mama who first said
What about Jade?
when Aunt Viney had to go back
to the Byberry State Hospital.
It was the fourth time in half a dozen years.

It was Mama who said Uncle Harold
belonged there himself
because all his people was peculiar
especially his mother who was Sanctified
and didn't eat pork or nothing
and didn't believe in doctors or anything
just like my father's mother (and most of his people)
and such a house
couldn't be no good for the child.
So it was Mama
who first took pity
and not Dad.

If Mama came back from church
with Aunt Viney
(who was on some kind of a probation
and living again with her peculiar husband)
and signified she could stay for lunch,
my father would get up from the radio,
leave the house without saying
more than hello
and not come back til past my bedtime.
Then he would have to warm up his own
dinner and get dressed
for the eleven o'clock shift.

But then Aunt Viney
had some kind of a relapse
and Mama went to get little Jade
out of that house
of old folks, Sanctified, and looking
like slaves. Making even that child
look old.
Mama dressed her up in my old clothes
which wasn't raggedy or anything
(Mama being so hard on me)
and we wasn't getting any help
from the court then.

And Mama coated her face with Noxema,
to get rid of the ash.
And Mama combed and brushed her hair
as much as three times a day
because it needed
a lot of training.

But then we started getting help from the court,
and my father's brothers and sisters
started coming around.
They started getting very tight.
And Mama signified nasty about it.
But when they were gone, my father said
Don't push me, Emma.
Don't push.
Everybody knows Viney is the biggest fool
always crying, always crying and going off —
colored people got better things to do!
A grown colored woman making herself
crazy over the dead —— Plenty people die!
What she think she is —— white?
What she got to be screaming for?
Mama is dead. Period.
And isn't she dead counting on God?

And Mama only said
that Aunt Viney was too young to be
so Sanctified
and she wasn't even
a bad-looking girl, at that.

knock on wood

HENRY DUMAS

i go out to totem street
    we play
    neon monster
        and watusi feet

killer sharks chasin behind
    we play hide
    siren!
        and out-run cops
they catch
    willie
    and me
        splittin over fence
they knock
    in willie's head
    hole
they kick me watusi
    down
        for dead
like yesterday
    runnin feet in my brain
    won't stop willie lookin blood
        beggin me
cut off blackjack pain

so whenever you see me comin
    crazy watusi
        you call me watusi
i keep a wooden willie
    blade and bone outa that fence
a high willie da conqueror
    listen! up there he talkin
wooden willie got all the sense

i go out to siren street
    don't play no more
me and willie beat a certain beat
    aimin wood carvin shadows

sometimes i knock on wood
    with fist
me and willie play *togetherin*
    and we don't miss

Untitled I

ISHMAEL REED

friday in berkeley. the crippled
ship has just returned frm
behind the moon . fools wave
flags on destroyers in the pacific
i am worried abt this dog
lying in the street . he wants
to get some sun . the old man
across the street trims his
rosebush while just 4 blocks
away there is a war . people
are being arraigned
fingerprinted
hauled away to st rita
made to lie on the floor
the newspapers will lie
abt all this . abt these
12 year olds throwing
stones at the cops . they
wanted to get at some sun
no matter what heavy
traffic was coming down
on them

"O.D."

ZACK GILBERT

These are also
The war victims,
These needle addicts
Dead at morning age.
Battles are fought
With more than
Guns and bullets;
An over dose
Of horse is just
As lethal.

So know
This enemy too
You once bright,
Quick eyed
Youths who
Droop and nod.
Turn from this
Death/sleep.

Junior Addict

LANGSTON HUGHES

The little boy
who sticks a needle in his arm
and seeks an out in other worldly dreams,
who seeks an out in eyes that droop
and ears that close to Harlem screams,
cannot know, of course,
(and has no way to understand)

a sunrise that he cannot see
beginning in some other land—
but destined sure to flood—and soon—
the very room in which he leaves
his needle and his spoon,
the very room in which today the air
is heavy with the drug
of his dispair.

       (Yet little can
       tomorrow's sunshine give
       to one who will not live.)

Quick, sunrise, come—
Before the mushroom bomb
Pollutes his stinking air
With better death
Than is his living here,
With viler drugs
Than bring today's release
In poison from the fallout
Of our peace.

       "It's easier to get dope
       than it is to get a job."

Yes, easier to get dope
than to get a job—
daytime or nightime job,
teen-age, pre-draft,
pre-lifetime job.

Quick, sunrise, come!
Sunrise out of Africa,
Quick, come!
Sunrise, please come!
Come! Come!

don't wanna be

SONIA SANCHEZ

don't wanna be
no pimp
        cuz pimps hate me and you
        they mommas, women, sistuhs too
        u name it, any hate will do

don't wanna be no pimp no mo
don't wanna be no pimp no mo

don't wanna be
no numbers runner
        cuz runner promise an uptown hit
        while downtown wite/boys just sit & sit
        while counting millions of four bits

don't wanna be no numbers runner no mo
don't wanna be no numbers runner no mo

don't wanna be
no junkie
        cuz junkies kill theyselves, you and me
        sticking needles in they arms, legs, knee
        while robbing our black community

don't wanna be no junkie no mo
don't wanna be no junkie no mo

Just wanna be
        a/Reverend/Cleage/man
        a/Minister/Farrakhan/man
        a/sun/people/Imamu/man
        an/Elijah/Muhammad/Messenger/man

wanna be
> a/blk/man
> a/loving/my blk/woman/man
> a/standing/still/Father/man
> a/Constant/T C Bing/black man

it gots to beeeEEE. yeah. yeah. yeah.
it gots to beeeEEE. yeah. yeah. yeah.

To My Daughter the Junkie on a Train
AUDRE LORDE

Children we have not borne
bedevil us by becoming
themselves
painfully sharp and unavoidable
like a needle in our flesh.

Coming home on the subway from a PTA meeting
of minds committed like murder
or suicide
to their own private struggle
a long-legged girl with a horse in her brain
slumps down beside me
begging to be ridden asleep
for the price of a midnight train
free from desire.
Little girl on the nod
if we are measured by the dreams we avoid
then you are the nightmare
of all sleeping mothers
rocking back and forth
the dead weight of your arms
locked about our necks

heavier than our habit
of looking for reasons.

My corrupt concern will not replace
what you once needed
but I am locked into my own addictions
and offer you my help, one eye
out
for my own station.
Roused and deprived
your costly dream explodes
into a terrible technicoloured laughter
at my failure
up and down across the aisle
women avert their eyes
as the other mothers who became useless
curse their children who became junk.

To Desi as Joe as Smoky the Lover of 115th Street

AUDRE LORDE

Who are you
that your name comes
broken by the speeding cars along the East Side Drive
tumbling out of the concrete wall flowers
as I pass
Desi as Joe as Smoky the Lover of 115th Street?

There was nothing furtive about the swirls
of neon-bright magenta
prancing off your fingertips
like ideal selves
is the dream you
valued more

because you glanced over your shoulder
as you wrote
the first letter
undecided
its flourish
shaped like a question mark?

But there was nothing at all
to see over your shoulder
except my eyes in a passing tide of cars
wondering
if you wrote under a culvert
so the approaching storm around us
would not wash you away.

There was nothing at all
furtive
about your magenta scrawling
but I saw the bright sweat
running off your childhood's face
as you glanced behind you
choosing that wall beneath a bridge
where so many others had written
before
that the colours merged into
one sunlit mosaic
face without name
decorating a highway
on the very edge of Manhattan.

Those Boys That Ran Together

LUCILLE CLIFTON

those boys that ran together
at Tillman's
and the poolroom
everybody see them now
think it's a shame

everybody see them now
remember they was fine boys

we have some fine black boys

don't it make you want to cry?

listen children

LUCILLE CLIFTON

listen children
keep this in the place
you have for keeping
always
keep it all ways

we have never hated black

listen
we have been ashamed
hopeless   tired   mad
but always
all ways
we loved us

we have always loved each other
children   all ways

pass it on

True Love

Friend

GWENDOLYN BROOKS

Walking with you
shuts off shivering.
Here we are.
Here we are.

I am with you to share and to bear and to care.

This is warm.
I want you happy, I want you warm.

Your Friend for our forever is what I am.
Your Friend in thorough thankfulness.

It is the evening of our love.
Evening is hale and whole.
Evening shall not go out.
Evening is comforting flame.
Evening is comforting flame.

Horses Graze

GWENDOLYN BROOKS

Cows graze.
Horses graze.
They
eat
eat
eat.

Their graceful heads
are bowed
bowed
bowed
in majestic oblivion.
They are nobly oblivious
to your follies,
your inflation,
the knocks and nettles of administration.
They
eat
eat
eat.
And at the crest of their brute satisfaction,
with wonderful gentleness, in affirmation,
they lift their clean calm eyes and they lie down
and love the world.
They speak with their companions.
They do not wish that they were otherwhere.
Perhaps they know that creature feet may press
only a few earth inches at a time,
that earth is anywhere earth,
that an eye may see,
wherever it may be,
the Immediate arc, alone, of life, of love.

A Black Wedding Song
First dedicated to
Charles and La Tanya,
Allen and Glenda,
Haki and Safisha.

GWENDOLYN BROOKS

I

This love is a rich cry over
the deviltries and the death.
A weapon-song. Keep it strong.

Keep it strong.
Keep it logic and Magic and lightning and Muscle.

Strong hand in strong hand, stride to
the Assault that is promised you (knowing
no armor assaults a pudding or a mush.)

Here is your Wedding Day.
Here is your launch.

Come to your Wedding Song.

II

For you
I wish the kindness that romps or sorrows along.
Or kneels.
I wish you the daily forgiveness of each other.
For war comes in from the World
and puzzles a darling duet—
tangles tongues,
tears hearts, mashes minds;
there will be the need to forgive.

I wish you jewels of black love.

Come to your Wedding Song.

Black Magic

DUDLEY RANDALL

Black girl black girl
lips as curved as cherries
full as grape bunches
sweet as blackberries

Black girl black girl
when you walk you are
magic as a rising bird
or a falling star

Black girl black girl
what's your spell to make
the heart in my breast
jump   stop   shake

Poem No. 21

DOUGHTRY LONG

if 'Trane had only seen
her body
and the way it smoothed
the brown light and
sent color to
the edge of darkness
as if it were the perfect
hands of some painter
he would have named it
with his horn
something vibrant and

unexplored, something loud
and still as someone
first touching their blackness.

One Time Henry Dreamed the Number
DOUGHTRY LONG

one time henry dreamed the number
but we didn't play it,
and do you know, that thing came out straight
3-67?
   yes it did!
we was both sick
for a whole week,
     could'a sure used
           the money then too.

that was back in hoover's time
when folks was scufflin
to make ends meet.
i knock on wood though
        we've lived through it all.

last night after we ate
the last of the meat loaf and greens
and was watching television
henry asked me if i remembered that,
i told him yes,
    we laughed
   then went to bed
and kept each other warm.

For Mattie & Eternity

STERLING D. PLUMPP

Thinking is not a smile
This morning
As I lay dry
Away from rivers welded in memory
Like twisted wires of sin
In a little boy's head
Lie awakening to you,
Mattie, Grand Morning of my dreams
Distance and time have foiled
My heart's waves against
Thanks to the sea
You poured through Mary
Into me, dancing like Black Angels
To music James Brown
Done holied hot
For my life is laughter
Only when my embrace
In your rhythms
Announces a thundering with feelings
Those seeingeyes tapping a beat
That unrivals heads and hearts
To teach love as a stream
Sanctified in prophecies
Running from Grandmother's hands
Down to God's listening ears . . .

When Sue Wears Red

LANGSTON HUGHES

When Susanna Jones wears red
Her face is like an ancient cameo
Turned brown by the ages.

Come with a blast of trumpets,
  Jesus!

When Susanna Jones wears red
A queen from some time-dead Egyptian night
Walks once again.

Blow trumpets, Jesus!

And the beauty of Susanna Jones in red
Burns in my heart a love-fire sharp like pain.

Sweet silver trumpets,
  Jesus!

Trellie

LANCE JEFFERS

From the old slave shack I chose my lady,
from the harsh garden of the South,
from the South's black children,
from the old slaves bending between the rows of cotton,
from Charlie James whose soul was African in
    the unredeeming Southern sun,
from the song of slaves who choked the sky like
    chitlins down their throats,
from the woman dark who stood and leaned back as

Southern women do, her stomach out, her shoulders
    back,
and wombed the grandeur of her poetry in song as
long and deep as prehistoric night,
in song as causeful as the fiery center of the earth,
in love as muscular as the thighs of
darkskinned god who cradled Africa to his chest,
in love as nippled as the milk that flows from Nile to sea:

She lies beside me in the night
    who is the greatness of the slaves without their fear,
she is the anger of this day and elegant pride
    that touched the child who walked three miles to
    school and saw white children's bus leave her trampling
    in the dust:

There is a beauty here that I aspire:
there is a grandeur here that I require:
the Southern loam to throw into the sandbags of my soul:
some other rapture that my song must lyre,
some woolier head to batter the entombment of my fire:
to lay my stunted heart upon the pyre and blow upon
    my godliness till it come down my mouth,
    the soul of my grandfather's sire
    when he stood harried in slavery.

As I lie beside her in the night I see America's
    birth in death
and tyranny grind its knife to seek my veins,
I see myself in prison camp alone,
hooking the guillotine's eye to my neckflesh when
    morning comes,
and she weeping and engrieved within my breast.

What more marrowed sorrow could there be
when tear large as blackness' pyramid will lodge my eye
    and drop, when my blood prepares to sink beneath
    the soil?

But Trellie's kin
　　will run the reindeer down from frozen North
and bring her love to me within my grave,
to all my whiter crimes and grudging heart,
to all my assasination of myself, and all my unyielding
　　hatred of tyranny.
All my children's New World conquering will grow like
　　elephant tusks from earth I drench in blood:
ten thousand children will redwood from my genes
　　to mount the earth in my black people's time!

Instructions to a princess
For tim

ISHMAEL REED

it is like the plot of an ol
novel. yr mother comes down
from the attic at midnite & tries
on weird hats. i sit in my study
the secret inside me. i deal it
choice pieces of my heart. down
in the village they gossip abt
the new bride.
i have been saving all this
love for you my dear. if my
house burns down, open my face
& you will be amazed.

They Live in Parallel Worlds

WILLIAM J. HARRIS

They live
in parallel
worlds
His is matter
Hers anti-matter

If they merely
hold hands
the universe
will explode

They find
a door
to a field
that links
the worlds

They can meet
in this Eden
if they stand
at opposite
ends

He shows her
a lilac
he picked
for her
in his world

She smiles
as the fragrance
slowly drifts
across the field

He
hopes
the scent
won't destroy
the universe

Coda

FRED JOHNSON

always there's some boy
                    meeting a girl
turning looks into love
        warmth into generations
a race builds on that
crawls outside itself
                    cranks up energy and
moves   builds   renews   moves

a race begins there
        begins after years of sifting
sun   wind   dark   fire   flood   spear   wheel   gun
        drops down through guilt
                            sinks whispering
shrinking in on itself
joy and terror mixing in the mouth
                            growing odors
that fill clothes when no more is left but
clothes
    fill nights with the terrible darkness
of uncertainty

a generation catches hold there
                            dances
in a stuttering heart beat

roots down deep into the flesh
                              grafts itself
jumps back behind the eyes
                              humming in its newness
and pushes   shaking itself loose from
the sigh.

Noises

  The eternal silence of these
  Infinite spaces
                    frightens me
                    — Pascal

  FRED JOHNSON

I want to write a poem
                    for you
that will sound
                    feel like the little electric tingles
skittering over my skin when I think your name
I want to tug
          pull your face to smiles
                              when you read the words

I want to write a poem
                    that will shimmer
and stand against your mind like yesterdays
I want to make visions
that will rage through your dreams
I want miles and miles of me
                              living inside you
racing with your blood
                    a poem of you coming
jumping into my life
               your eyes calm

and your voice
            like a vanishing summer storm
rolling around in me.

I want to find noisy things
                    to fill the void
I want to jam the silence
                    of these spaces
with our whispers   our laughter
I want to fill the emptiness with our eye
                            mind contact
I want the feeling to slide between us in waves
smothering distance
                stifling fears
                        exploding the vacuum
tall sounds
        of people living
small sounds
            feathering
                billowing vibrating
connecting youtometoyoutometo
                        you to me
                            to you.

poem

PEARL CLEAGE LOMAX

you said.
don't write me
a love poem,
but i would like to
creep across
yr shoulder and

whisper poems into
yr ear.
soft and black
moist and black
beautiful and black-
Strong.
rubbing my body
against yr chest.
Black.
and when you
ask me
why
i am so quiet.
it is only because
the poem sits
smiling
just
behind my lips.

A Certain Peace

NIKKI GIOVANNI

it was very pleasant
not having you around
this afternoon

not that i don't love you
and want you and need you
and love loving and wanting and needing you

but there was a certain peace
when you walked out the door
and i knew you would do something
you wanted to do
and i could run

a tub full of water
and not worry about answering the phone
for your call
and soak in bubbles
and not worry whether you would want something
special for dinner
and rub lotion all over me
for as long as i wanted
and not worry if you had a good idea
or wanted to use the bathroom

and there was a certain excitement
when after midnight you came home
and we had coffee
and i had a day of mine
that made me as happy
as yours did you

[9 jan 72]

Your Eyes Have Their Silence

GERALD W. BARRAX

Your eyes have their silence in giving words
back more beautifully than trees can rain
and give back in swaying the rain
that makes silence mutable and startles nesting birds.

And so it rains. And so I speak or not
as your eyes go from silence suddenly
at love to wonder (as those quiet birds suddenly
at rain) letting, finally, myself be taught

silence before your eyes conceding everything
spoken as experience, as love, as reason
enough not to speak of them and my reason
crawls into the silence of your eyes. Spring

If She Sang

GERALD W. BARRAX

I would worry less if she sang:
   in the kitchen amid the harvest of noise
   she sows around her like dragon's teeth;
   or in the corner of our room
   where she stitches to herself
   quietly except when she
                   bursts into speech
so far from both of us
a third person is its only medium.
Sometimes I answer,
knowing the risk of being told
a body should be able to talk to itself in peace,
knowing no alarm that brings someone who loves us
is false,
knowing she may send other ways to bring me.
   I would worry
   less
   if she sang:
I understand song
and could go uninvited
into that world
but in her moments of self and
                   counter
self
   are dimensions with room
   for only two

Morning Song

HENRY BLAKELY

I do not need a springtime,
or place apart, to love you.
I need no cloak of night, no starmoon
silvered on a sea.

I love you in the rain, and when
we're washing dishes after supper.
I love you moving, sleeping, talking.
You being, I love.

Music you are and mostly
bright May weather. I love you
twice the numbered sands of deserts
and lengths of beaches.

Ballad of the Morning Streets

AMIRI BARAKA (LEROI JONES)

The magic of the day is the morning
I want to say the day is morning high
and sweet, good
morning.

The ballad of the morning streets, sweet
voices turns
of cool warm weather
high around the early windows grey to blue
and down again amongst the kids and
broken signs, is pure love magic, sweet day
come into me, let me live with you
and dig your blazing

Tight Rope

AMIRI BARAKA (LEROI JONES)

We live in fragments
like speech. Like the fits
of wind, shivering against
the window.

Pieces of meaning, pierced
and strung together. The bright bead
of the poem, the bright bead
of your woman's laughter.

LOVE TIGHT

TED JOANS

PLACE YOUR HAND
INTO MY HAND AND

OPEN YOUR MOUTH
WIDE AS MY MOUTH

AND CLOSE YOUR EYES
AS TIGHT AS YOU CAN

THEN IMAGINE WE
BOTH ARE TWO

LIONS IN LOVE
FOREVER

Anna

JOE JOHNSON

Little anna   brown anna
time on mind anna time on wrist anna
good anna soft brown anna giggle anna
brown anna good anna brown anna
time mind anna time on face
anna anna anna anna

True Love

JOE JOHNSON

This morning   I held Harriet in my head against an orange
        cloud
I held Harriet until my lips burned

Myself When I Am Real

poem at thirty

SONIA SANCHEZ

it is midnight
no magical bewitching
hour for me
i know only that
i am here waiting
remembering that
once as a child
i walked two
miles in my sleep.
did i know
then where i
was going?
traveling. i'm
always traveling.
i want to tell
you about me
about nights on a
brown couch when
i wrapped my
bones in lint and
refused to move.
no one touches
me anymore.
father do not
send me out
among strangers
you you black man
stretching scraping
the mold from your body.
here is my hand.
i am not afraid
of the night.

present

SONIA SANCHEZ

this woman vomiten her
  hunger over the world
this melancholy woman forgotten
before memory came
  this yellow movement bursten forth like
Coltrane's melodies all mouth
  buttocks moven like palm trees,
this honeycoatedalabamianwoman
raining rhythms of blue / blk / smiles
this yellow woman carryen beneath her breasts
  pleasures without tongues
  this woman whose body weaves
  desert patterns,
this woman, wet with wanderen,
reviven the beauty of forests and winds
is tellen u secrets
gather up yo odors and listen
as she sings the mold from memory

        there is no place
for a soft / blk / woman
there is no smile green enough or
summertime words warm enough to allow my growth
and in my head
i see my history
standen like a shy child
and i chant lullabies
as i ride my past on horseback
tasten the thirst of yesterday tribes
hearen the ancient / blk / woman

me singen hay - hay
        hay - hay - hay - ya - ya - ya
        hay - hay - hay
        hay - hay - ya - ya - ya
                                like a slow scent
beneath the sun
                and i dance my
creation and my grandmother's gatheren
from my bones like great wooden birds
spread their wings
while their long / legged / laughter /
stretches the night.
                and i taste the
seasons of my birth. mangoes, papayas
drink my woman / coconut / milks
stalk the ancient grandfathers
sippen on proud afternoons
walk with a song round my waist
tremble like a new / born / child troubled
with new breaths
                and my singen
becomes the only sound of a
blue / blk / magical / woman. walken.
womb ripe. walken. loud with mornings. walken
maken pilgrimage to herself. walken.

Give Me Five

In all things that are purely social we can be
as separate as the fingers, yet one as the hand
in all things essential to mutual progress.
                  — Booker T. Washington

WILLIAM J. HARRIS

I can't talk
outuva car
to the passing blood

My "What's
happenin"
is a little flat

My "man"
is
self-conscious

My five is
more like
four

I guess I ain't
a very natural
brother

High on the Hog

JULIA FIELDS

Take my share of Soul Food —
I do not wish
To taste of pig
  Of either gut
    Or grunt
    From bowel
      Or jowl

I want caviar
Shrimp soufflé
Sherry
  Champagne
    And not because
   Whites' domain
   But just because
   I'm entitled —

For I've been
    V.d.'d enough
    T.b.'d enough
   and
  Hoe-cake fed Knock-Knee'd enough
  Spindly led bloodhound tree'd enough
     To eat
     High on the Hog

I've been
    Hired last
    Fired first enough

I've sugar-watered my
    Thirst enough —

Been lynched enough
          Slaved enough
          Cried enough
          Died enough

Been deprived—
          Have survived enough
               To eat
High on the Hog.
Keep the black-eyed peas
     And the grits,
     The high blood-pressure chops
     And gravy sops

I want aperitifs supreme
               Baked Alaska—
          Something suave, cool
          For I've been considered faithful fool
          From 40 acres and a mule . . .

I've been
          Slighted enough
          Sever-righted enough
          And up tighted enough
     And I want
          High on the Hog

For dragging the cotton sack
          On bended knees
          In burning sun
          In homage to the
               Great King cotton
          For priming the money-green tobacco
               And earning pocket-change

     For washing in iron pots
     For warming by coal and soot
     For eating the leavings from
          Others' tables

I've lived my wretched life
          Between domestic rats
                    And foreign wars
          Carted to my final rest
                    In second-hand cars

But I've been leeched enough
          Dixie-peached enough
          Color bleached enough

                    And I want
                    High on the Hog!

Oh, I've heard the Mau Maus
          Screaming

                    Romanticizing Pain
          I hear them think
          They go against the Grain

But I've lived in shacks
                    Long enough
          Had strong black beaten
                    Backs long enough

And I've been
          Urban-planned
                    Been Moynihanned
          Enough
          And I want
          High on the Hog

For Black Poets Who Think of Suicide
ETHERIDGE KNIGHT

Black Poets should live — not leap
From steel bridges, like the white boys do.

Black Poets should *live* — not lay
Their necks on railroad tracks, (like the white boys do.
Black Poets should seek, but not search
Too much in sweet dark caves
Or hunt for snipes down psychic trails —
(Like the white boys do;

For Black Poets belong to Black People.
Are the flutes of Black Lovers — Are
The organs of Black Sorrows — Are
The trumpets of Black Warriors.
Let all Black Poets die as trumpets,
And be buried in the dust of marching feet.

For Poets

AL YOUNG

Stay beautiful
but dont stay down underground too long
Dont turn into a mole
or a worm
or a root
or a stone

Come on out into the sunlight
Breathe in trees
Knock out mountains
Commune with snakes
& be the very hero of birds

Dont forget to poke your head up
& blink
think
Walk all around
Swim upstream

Dont forget to fly

beware: do not read this poem

ISHMAEL REED

tonite, *thriller* was
abt an ol woman, so vain she
surrounded her self w/
   many mirrors

it got so bad that finally she
locked herself indoors & her
whole life became the
   mirrors

one day the villagers broke
into her house, but she was too
swift for them. she disappeared
    into a mirror
each tenant who bought the house
after that, lost a loved one to
    the ol woman in the mirror:
    first a little girl
    then a young woman
    then the young woman/s husband

the hunger of this poem is legendary
it has taken in many victims
back off from this poem
it has drawn in yr feet
back off from this poem
it has drawn in yr legs
back off from this poem
it is a greedy mirror
you are into this poem. from
   the waist down
nobody can hear you can they?
this poem has had you up to here
    belch

this poem aint got no manners
you cant call out frm this poem
relax now & go w/ this poem
move & roll on to this poem

        do not resist this poem
        this poem has yr eyes
        this poem has his head
        this poem has his arms
        this poem has his fingers
        this poem has his fingertips

        this poem is the reader & the
        reader this poem

statistic: the us bureau of missing persons reports
        that in 1968 over 100,000 people disappeared
        leaving no solid clues
                nor trace   only
a space   in the lives of their friends

The Reactionary Poet

ISHMAEL REED

If you are a revolutionary
Then I must be a reactionary
For if you stand for the future
I have no choice but to
Be with the past

Bring back suspenders!
Bring back Mom!
Homemade ice cream
Picnics in the park
Flagpole sitting

Straw hats
Rent parties
Corn liquor
The banjo
Georgia quilts
Krazy Kat
Restock
The syncopation of
Fletcher Henderson
The Kiplingesque lines
Of James Weldon Johnson
Black Eagle
Mickey Mouse
The Bach Family
Sunday School
Even Mayor LaGuardia
Who reads the comics
Is more appealing than
Your version of
What Lies Ahead

In your world of
Tomorrow Humor
Will be locked up and
The key thrown away
The public address system
Will pound out headaches
All day
Everybody will wear the same
Funny caps
And the same funny jackets

Enchantment will be found
Expendable, charm, a
Luxury
Love and kisses
A crime against the state

Duke Ellington will be
Ordered to write more marches

"For the people," naturally

If you are what's coming
I must be what's going

Make it by steamboat
I likes to take it real slow

Survivor

JUDY DOTHARD SIMMONS

I grow
I see
nothing was ever mine nor will ever be mine
my only property
is what is left of myself
after I take off intellect
like a dress I have grown too small for;
after love drops from my feet like raggedy slippers
I scuffed through some alien house in
for years;
after ethics become as flaccid as the oversize Playtex gloves
I've used too long with ammonia
trying to scrub sludge off my stove

I don't even eat now;
the vitamins keep me going;
an occasional gift of fried fish
reminds me to wish Jesus luck
on his second coming

the cigarettes are left,
and glasses of chilled, sterile water,
four cats that are my anchors,
and the absence of despair
that nothing was ever mine
nor will ever be mine

I am vastly grateful
that I have become nearly empty;
I am kinder now and more ruthless;
I am gentle with broken men,
patient with grossly warped women

I stare dead straight into the cold blue eyes of existence
no longer frightened because they don't care

it's comforting

JUDY DOTHARD SIMMONS

it's comforting
to do what you do well
even if it isn't what you want to do
in the Hollywood places
of your head

reared for glamour fantasies,
mad from the drab reality,
raging at lies that sent
a filament of youthful heart
beyond the spangled galaxies of
song and glance and nuance of the camera,
the gossamer dance, slick brow arch flat-assed
Loretta Young
to be black and never to be
beautiful

it's comforting to do what you do well
dreams are for
/if it doesn't hurt too much/
o god
the dreaming

Where She Was Not Born

YVONNE

He built right on top of the land
without tree or rut
(believing sweat, a bootlick —
no salt of the earth;
believing moonshine, rain; his brass bed
collateral enough).
Rhino thick
in thought, tongue, and tool
he built
turtle squat,
low as a pregnant sow,
a wood and scrap brick bungalow
on short stout legs.

And she said:
"You ain't got the stillness
for digging — let alone the claws.
You ain't got the flesh,
just useless fever."
And every day she prayed
at the table of pinch and save,
rose from the feast
cursed his meatless gut,
his unbaptized garrulousness,

that he had built
where she could hardly root,
let alone glorify her wings.

A Common Poem

CAROLYN M. RODGERS

seasons/changes moods
the things of this earth
are the things that give us pleasure.
the sunset and glow, the rise . . .
the grass blue or green, thin or tall
yet growing
the common flowers or special
the sky blue or gray smiling or sad
the air warm or wet, cold wind and wild
or sweet and careful to the feel,
a loving
touch.
these seasons are the things we love
the rhythm that keeps us moving
together or alone we take it or share it—
the things of this earth
are the things that give us pleasure.

Some Me of Beauty

CAROLYN M. RODGERS

    the fact is
that i don't hate any body any more
    i went through my mean period
    if you remember i spit out nails
      chewed tobacco on the paper
and dipped some bad snuff.
    but in one year
just like i woke up one morning and
    saw my mother's head gray
and i asked myself/could it have turned
    overnight?
knowing full well the grayness had been
    coming and had even been there
    awhile
just like that i woke up one morning
  and looked at my self
    and what i saw was
            carolyn
    not imani ma jua or soul sister poetess of
      the moment
    i saw more than a "sister" . . .
      i saw a Woman. human.
            and black.
    i felt a spiritual transformation
      a root revival of love
    and i knew that many things
      were   over
    and some me of — beauty —
            was about to begin. . . .

how i got ovah

CAROLYN M. RODGERS

i can tell you
about them
i have shaken rivers
out of my eyes
i have waded eyelash deep
have crossed rivers
have shaken the water weed out
of my lungs
have swam for strength
pulled by strength
through waterfalls with electric beats
i have bore the shocks
of water deep deep
waterlogs are my bones
i have shaken the water free of my hair
have kneeled on the banks
and kissed my ancestors of the dirt
whose rich dark root fingers rose up reached out
grabbed and pulled me rocked me cupped me
gentle strong and firm
carried me
made me swim for strength
cross rivers
though i shivered
was wet was cold
and wanted to sink down
and float as water, yea—
I can tell you.
I have shaken rivers
out of my eyes.

Terra Cotta

K. CURTIS LYLE

the nose becomes a triangular history
of the soul,
passion and the expressive stillness
of eternity
circular and flat-out
the eyes extend outward
into the galaxies
and inward toward
the muscle waters
of red chord and created wood
incanted to crest and wavelength, undying
and undeniable flesh
hardened into an infinite caress,
the indifferent malaise
of change rolling unnoticed,
invisible tangent marked by everything,
the washer-woman of love's elusive interiors
marked by nothing
but subversive and seditious spiritual pock marks,
silver hair circumsized
where it once disappeared into the void
of polychrome
strange medicinal
and penitential halos,
terra cotta,
petrified wood broken under the aegis
of radium and laser

the instant
of this passion
the insistence
of this presence,

survival of what we mean to be the truth
does not mean what we say or feel
in that secret portion
                    of our selves
is really going to be the truth,
does not mean
that what survives
                    of our secret selves
or what we feel most at ease in
is really going to be the truth,
does not mean that these words
are really going to speak the truth
or even pretend to know what that pestilential
word
really means
does not mean that our mouths
are any less grotesque
than the word of God,
but only means that mouths
do not come
as wide as the wind wonder working
on the world's plain,
has no alternative but creation
of the diametric
by the diametrically opposed,
is a narrow slit, a minuscule crack
in the great black wall
                    of the universe

When We Hear the Eye Open . . .

BOB KAUFMAN

When we hear the eye open, there, in that place,
There, a whisper is a scream,
Breathing there, in that place,
A breath is the birth of sound,
We shall see our reflections
On the gigantic thighs of a giant,
There, in that place,
My head is a bony guitar, strung with tongues, plucked by fingers &
        nails,
The giant is only his legs, the rest of him will be gone far on,
And blinking cities will fly from his knees,
    And in a future, in that place, there,
        I was a nut in a chocolate bar,
            And I melted in a soft hand,
                And we sang a luna tune,

The ear hears fear, the eye lies, the mind dies, the teeth curl,
And Runic stone alone, weeps at the death of sleep,
Colder than a frozen nun, chilly accusations point,
Naked river, screamer on lonely poet corners,
Yes, and bugs with lights another crime of mine
How else walk against these black winds of mind death,
Blowing down these lonely streets,
They have found a way to disturb the moon,
The sun burns at love's two ends,
On the eternal launching pad.

Unholy Missions

BOB KAUFMAN

I want to be buried in an anonymous crater inside the moon.

I want to build miniature golf courses on all the stars.

I want to prove that Atlantis was a summer resort for cave men.

I want to prove that Los Angeles is a practical joke played on us by superior beings on a humorous planet.

I want to expose Heaven as an exclusive sanitarium filled with rich psychopaths who think they can fly.

I want to show that the Bible was serialized in a Roman children's magazine.

I want to prove that the sun was born when God fell asleep with a lit cigarette, tired after a hard night of judging.

I want to prove once and for all that I am not crazy.

Scrapbooks

NIKKI GIOVANNI

it's funny that smells and sounds return
so all alone uncalled unneeded
on a sweaty night as i sit armed
with coffee and cigarettes waiting

sometimes it seems
my life is a scrapbook

i usta get 1.50 per week

for various duties unperformed
while i read *green dolphin street*
and *the sun is my undoing*
never understanding my exclusion
but knowing quite clearly the hero
is always misunderstood
though always right in the end

roy gave me a yellow carnation
that year for the junior prom

the red rose was from michael
who was the prettiest boy i'd ever known
he took me to the *jack and jill* dance
and left me sitting in the corner until
the slow drags came on then he danced
real tight and sweated out my bangs

i had a white leather monstrosity that passed
for taste in my adolescence pressed with dances
undanced though the songs were melodious

and somehow three or four books were filled
with proms and parties and programs that
my grandmother made me go to
for "culture" so that i could be
a lady
my favorite is the fisk book with clippings
of the *forum* and notes from the dean of women
saying "you are on social probation" and "you are
suspended from fisk"
and letters from my mother saying "behave yourself"
and letters from my grandmother reminding me
"your grandfather graduated fisk in 1905" and not
to try to run the school
but mostly notes from alvin asking when
was i coming over
again
i purchased a blue canvas notebook for the refrain

it's really something when you sit
watching dawn peep over apartment buildings
that seemed so ominous during the night and see
pages of smiling pictures   groups of girls throwing
pillows   couples staring nervously ahead as if they
think the kodak will eat them   someone with a ponytail
and a miles davis record   a lady with an afro pointing
joyously to a diploma   a girl in a brown tan and red
bathing suit holding a baby that looks like you

and now there is a black leather book filled
efficiently by a clipping service
and a pile of unanswered letters that remind
you to love those who love you
and i sit at dawn
all my defenses gone sometimes
listening to *something cool* sometimes
hearing *tears on my pillow*
and know there must be other books
filled with failures and family and friends
that perhaps one day i can unfold
for my grandchildren

        [11 dec 71]

[Untitled]
For Margaret Danner

NIKKI GIOVANNI

one ounce of truth benefits
like ripples on a pond
one ounce of truth benefits like a ripple
on a pond
one ounce of truth

benefits like ripples on
a pond
as things change remember my smile

the old man said my time is getting near
the old man said my time
is getting near
he looked at his dusty cracked boots to say
sister my time is getting near
and when i'm gone remember i smiled
when i'm gone remember
i smiled
i'm glad my time is getting there

the baby cried wanting some milk
the baby cried needing some milk
the baby he cried for wanting
his mother kissed him gently

when i came they sang a song
when i was born they sang a song
when i was saved they sang a song
remember i smiled when i'm gone
remember i smiled when i'm gone
sing a good song when i'm gone
we ain't got long to stay

[28 feb 72]

Probability and Birds

RUSSELL ATKINS

The probability in the yard:
The rodent keeps the cat close by;
The cat would sharp at the bird;

The bird would waft to the water—
If he does he has but his times before.
Whichever one he is   he's surely marked

The cat is variable
The rodent becomes the death of the bird
Which we love
                    dogs are random

After the Killing

DUDLEY RANDALL

"We will kill,"
said the blood-thirster,
"and after the killing
there will be peace."

But after the killing
their sons
killed his sons,

and his sons
killed their sons,

and their sons
killed his sons

until

at last

a blood-thirster said,
"We will kill.
And after the killing
there will be   peace."

The Raising of Lazarus
LUCILLE CLIFTON

the dead shall rise again.
whoever say
dust must be dust,
don't see the trees
smell rain
remember Africa.
everything that goes
can come.
stand up!
even the dead shall rise.

Leadbelly Gives an Autograph
AMIRI BARAKA (LEROI JONES)

Pat your foot
and turn
       the corner. Nat Turner, dying wood
of the church. Our lot
is vacant. Bring the twisted myth
of speech. The boards brown and falling
away. The metal bannisters cheap
and rattly. Clean new Sundays. We thought
it possible to enter
the way of the strongest.

But it is rite that the world's ills
erupt as our own. Right that we take
our own specific look into the shapely
blood of the heart.

          Looking thru trees
the wicker statues blowing softly against
the dusk.
Looking thru dusk
thru dark-
ness. A clearing of stars
and half-soft mud.

The possibilities of music. First
that it does exist. And that we do,
in that scripture of rhythms. The earth,
I mean the soil, as melody. The fit you need,
the throes. To pick it up and cut
away what does not singularly express.

Need.
Motive.
The delay of language.

A strength to be handled by giants.

The possibilities of statement. I am saying, now,
what my father could not remember
to say. What my grandfather
was killed
for believing.
          Pay me off, savages.
          Build me an equitable human assertion.

One that looks like a jungle, or one that looks like the cities
of the West.   But I provide the stock. The beasts
and myths.
          The City's Rise!
               (And what is history, then? An
                   old deaf lady
                   burned to death
                   in South Carolina.)

Funeral Poem

AMIRI BARAKA (LEROI JONES)

In death the dead remember their spirit
selves and be with us in spirit for now
and here and not with us but near us forever
as they are
in their mist skin
in their fire, or air, or watery
substance
the dead are
with us always
not as the dead
but as the breath
not as the husk
but as the seed
they live
other places
they take
other faces
they are the living
they are the evolved beings

my love with them, is going, never
to leave me, dear lady i lost you
young child you are tomorrow
wait for me on the other side of appearance
wait for me near wet evening and dancing
near drums
and soft laughing
you are a voice in my self
a night a day a moment an eternity
a bright burst of light and holiness

were
ever

Lenox Christmas Eve 68

SAM CORNISH

Barns grow slowly out of the dark
Rain disappears in the night
Birds are building nests in dry and private places
Your tongue spits and clicks in sleep.

Some of us in laundromats eating
cold hamburgers watching the lonely small town roads
are covered with hundreds of years
and western skin.

One by one trees touch us.
I hear grass breaking in rabbits' teeth.

Sooner or Later

SAM CORNISH

sooner or later
somebody dies
in your family
& you got to know
what to do
or you are going
to feel bad
when the women
pull out
their hankerchiefs
& your hands
are still
in your pockets

A Black Man

SAM CORNISH

a black man
in the water
stands
in sand and cold
stones
push on his feet
like any other man

did I expect something
different
because
we are another kind
of man

the first
and last
the one who the convoy
comes for
the new man in the ovens

Movement Song

AUDRE LORDE

I have studied the tight curls on the back of your neck
moving away from me
beyond anger or failure
your face in the evening schools of longing
through mornings of wish and ripen
we were always saying goodbye
in the blood in the bone over coffee

before dashing for elevators going
in different directions
without goodbyes

Do not remember me as a bridge or a roof
as a maker of legends
nor as the trap door to a world
where black and white clericals
hang on the edges of beauty in 5 o'clock elevators
twitching their shoulders
to avoid each others flesh
and now
there is someone to speak for them
moving away from me into tomorrows
morning of wish and ripen
your goodbye is a promise of lightning
in the last angels hand unwelcome and warning
the sands have run out against us
we were rewarded by journeys away from each other
into desire and mornings alone
where excuse and endurance mingle
conceiving decision.

Do not remember me as disaster
nor as the keeper of secrets
I am a fellow rider in the cattle car
watching
you move slowly out of my bed
saying we cannot waste time
only ourselves.

For My Unborn & Wretched Children

A. B. SPELLMAN

if i bring back
life to a home of want
let it be me.

let me be, if i come
back, new, hands in first,
the mouth in.

if hands & mouth are in,
the belly, filled, clothes
the body. *then* want.

if want & hurt are clothed, bring
back life to home. if
want decides, let it be me.

Myself When I Am Real
For Charles Mingus

AL YOUNG

The sun is shining in my backdoor
right now.
          I picture myself thru jewels
the outer brittleness gone as I
fold within always.   Melting.

Love of life is love of God
sustaining all life,
                    sustaining me
when wrong or un-self-righteous
in drunkenness & in peace.

                        He who loves me
is me. I shall return to Him always,
my heart is rain, my brain earth,
but there is only one sun & forever
it shines forth one endless poem
of which my ranting, my whole life
is but breath.

            I long to fade back
into this door of sun forever

Make Music with Your Life

Make Music with Your Life

BOB O'MEALLY

Make music with your life
a
   jagged
silver tune
cuts every deepday madness
Into jewels   that you wear

Carry 16 bars of old blues
wit/you
everywhere you go
walk thru azure sadness
howlin
Like a guitar player

Ray Charles

SAM CORNISH

do you
dig ray
charles

when the
blues are
silent

in his throat

& he rolls
up his
sleeves

The Bishop of Atlanta: Ray Charles

JULIAN BOND

The Bishop seduces the world with his voice
Sweat strangles mute eyes
As insinuations gush out through a hydrant of sorrow
Dreams, a world never seen
Moulded on Africa's anvil, tempered down home
Documented in cries and wails
Screaming to be ignored, crooning to be heard
Throbbing from the gutter
On Saturday night
Silver offering only
The Right Reverend's back in town
Don't it make you feel all right?

Blues Note

BOB KAUFMAN

Ray Charles is the black wind of Kilimanjaro,
Screaming up-and-down blues,
Moaning happy on all the elevators of my time.

Smiling into the camera, with an African symphony
Hidden in his throat, and *(I Got a Woman)* wails, too.

He burst from Bessie's crushed black skull
One cold night outside of Nashville, shouting,
And grows bluer from memory, glowing bluer, still.

At certain times you can see the moon
Balanced on his head.

From his mouth he hurls chunks of raw soul.

He separated the sea of polluted sounds
And led the blues into the Promised Land.

Ray Charles is a dangerous man ('way cross town),
And I love him.

for Ray Charles's birthday
N.Y.C./1961

How High the Moon

LANCE JEFFERS

(first the melody, clean and hard,
and the flat slurs are faint;
the downknotted mouth, tugged in deprecation,
is not there. But near the end of the first chorus
the slurs have come
with the street of the quiet pogrom:
the beat of the street talk flares strong,
the scornful laughter and the gestures cut the air.)

"Blow! Blow!" the side-men cry,

and the thin black young man with an old man's face
lungs up
the tissue of a trumpet from his deep-cancered corners,
racks out a high and searing curse!
        Full from the sullen grace of his street it sprouts:
                NEVER YOUR CAPTIVE!

Nina Simone

LANCE JEFFERS

this brown woman's voice,
this blackwheat voice
this blackthigh voice
this blackbreast voice:
far far in the dim of me I hear her in the dark field
    of the slavery South:
gowned in burlap, barefoot,
head down, a musing smile on her lips:
out into the fields before the dawn she goes alone:
she gazes into the trees swaying in the slowly-draining
    night:
sudden grief pierces her torso and she laughs scornfully:

Now she stands before a microphone and
    feels the echoes of her slavery past:
an ache across her torso and a desolating laugh:
she throws back her head to sing and her teeth whiten
    the bloodsea of her mouth.

Homage to the Empress of the Blues

ROBERT HAYDEN

Because there was a man somewhere in a candystripe silk shirt,
gracile and dangerous as a jaguar and because a woman moaned
for him in sixty-watt gloom and mourned him Faithless Love
Twotiming Love Oh Love Oh Careless Aggravating Love,

    She came out on the stage in yards of pearls, emerging like
    a favorite scenic view, flashed her golden smile and sang.

Because grey laths began somewhere to show from underneath
torn hurdygurdy lithographs of dollfaced heaven;
and because there were those who feared alarming fists of snow
on the door and those who feared the riot-squad of statistics,

    She came out on the stage in ostrich feathers, beaded satin,
    and shone that smile on us and sang.

Poem for Otis Redding
JOYCE CAROL THOMAS

Listening to the man
straight from
the Georgia woods
sitting on the Dock of the Bay
claiming Nobody Knows You When
You're Down and Out

I get high every time
he starts to climb
that sweet soul mountain
dusting the air
with steep gotta gotta gottas
and craggy uh uh uhs

Weeping some slow fast
rhymes of love
measuring out
the blues he's a lover
in lyrical madness

Hearing the guitar
screaming
way back inside of me
stirring, jumping

all over my mind
then clinging
to the very last summit
doing the Hucklebuck

The MJQ

JOYCE CAROL THOMAS

Solemn pastors
Majestic ministers in navy blue
Running up and down the elevators
Of my passion
Can you count the mysteries
Of the MJQ?

They're stopping
Between floors
What is that chord?

Riding down to the cellar
With Django sounds
I know I'll never
Rise again
Then Delicate pasticios
Say Travel a little higher

South African Bloodstone
For Hugh Masekela

QUINCY TROUPE

South African bloodstone
drenched with the soil
drenched with the beauty
of the drum-drum beat of land

drenched with the beauty
of God's first creation of man

& sculpted into lean hawk look
eyes burning deep
                    bold diamonds of fire
dance sing music to the air

Conjureman/conjure up
the rhythm of voodoo walk
weave the spell/paint the trance
begin the fire ritual

Hugh Masekela! homeboy
from the original home/going home
play your horn your trumpet horn
screech scream speak of ancestors

Conjureman/conjure up
the memory of ancestral lands
the easy walk the rhythmic walk
click click talk of trumpet genius

Hugh Masekela homeboy
from the original home going home

Speak South African bloodstone speak!

A Portrait of Rudy

OLUMO (JIM CUNNINGHAM)

He sits
among his drums
a sea among its shores
sits confident
not even distance outstretches
his reach
he sits
ruling the world
with a touch

his foot
touches the sand
kicking its ancient fires
into brighter heat

his foot
touches the sand
fondling its wetness
like a partially hidden moon
slightly sinking
into secret places
his gleaming mouth open
an idle sun
burns spaces
in his eyes
blessing them
with beach rooms of openness

as his mouth
reopens
with a laugh
as his wide nostrils
tease the cold water
with simmering scoops

of heaping sand

he stands
gleaming on the world
with his drums

Percussions

RON WELBURN

we have these drums
you know stretched
over the balafon earth
australia to haiti
bahia to harlem
kimberly to cairo
quick fingers slapping
under reeds flutes or horns
pharaoh's prayers vibrate
the diaphrammed world
from the eye of the universe
singing that is strange souls
nothing you or I heard from
guinea these new guinea melodies
this must be the way we first
raised our voices in celebration
this is the way our ancestors
hearts must have beat tight in breasts
this is the way ti-roro and potato
learned the immense depth of life itself
we speak our arms wrists palms and fingertips
gone beyond wearisome aching
we have this will of expression
you know drums and kinds of naked pianos
and horns beat on
brightly you know for song.

good times & no bread
for babs gonzales

REGINALD LOCKETT

we move very fast & smoothly
thru serious cities & states
down with the common cold or the
flu
we may not have the bread   &
we may be scufflin hard hard hard
but we got all the fun
cause our sounds got colors
& our colors got sounds
spaced out thru & beyond time
our immortal images/spirits
dance space dances
from way back in
dahomean ceremonial rites for some
good & powerful god like papa
legba always on his job at the
gate
all the way to some of them mean
nowtime steps & mystical variations
we be pullin off on
abstract invaders of
the apocalypse out to
snap the life lines to our
visions as we move at
safe speeds
down speedways tightly
sprinkled with signs that
tell us where & when to go
but our elders taught us the
signs
taught us
right from left

round from square
on from off   &
here from there
we are afro-spacemen travelin in
view of the mind's eye
psychic-hitmen ready to
melt the mental ice
celestial custodians who
brush away the spirit's frost
circuit riders
takin back streets to the
music & good times in these
articulate chess playin/trump holdin
cities & states

Effendi
For McCoy Tyner

MICHAEL S. HARPER

The piano hums
again the clear
story of our coming,
enchained, severed,
our tongues gone,
herds the quiet
musings of ten million
years blackening the earth
with blood and our moon women,
children we loved,
the jungle swept up
in our rhapsodic song
giving back
banana leaves and

the incessant beating
of our tom-tom hearts.
We have sung a long time here
with the cross and the cotton field.
Those white faces turned
away from their mythical
beginnings are no art
but that of violence—
the kiss of death.
Somewhere on the inside
of those faces
are the real muscles
of the world;
the ones strengthened
in experience and pain,
the ones wished for in one's lover
or in the mirror
near the eyes
that record this lost, dogged data
and is pure, new, even lovely
and is you.

Cannon Arrested

For Julian "Cannonball" Adderley

MICHAEL S. HARPER

Somethin' Else and
Kind of Blue
bleed back to back
as the Cannon arrests,
his V-shaped heart
flowing in glycerine
compounds of fixed signs

stabilized in his going:
who helps him as he softshoes
starstreamed joculars across
each throated arch of song,
stylings of separation?

His fat silent reed
beds down in Gary,
shanked by Stevie Wonderful's
moment of silence,
these mosquito whinings
near the liter can of gas
I pour into Buick 59.

In some unmarked Floridian grave
another ancestor shakes
to your damnation,
her son perhaps pulling a giant
sailboat behind his Cadillac
to sporty Idlewild, Michigan,
sanctified in attitudes
of "Dis Here" on this side of the road,
"Dat Dere" *going over* on that side,
and the boat docks before me
in distant transformed banks
of you transporting this evil
woman's song pianola-ed
on Interstate 80, cardiac bypass
road-turn you didn't make,
your fins sailing over boundaries,
lined fingerings in a reefered house,
a divided storehouse near a Black
resort town, this sweet alto-man
wickered in vestibule, drifting away.

Fall Down
In Memory of Eric Dolphy

CALVIN C. HERNTON

All men are locked in their cells.
Though we quake
In the fist of the body
Keys rattle, set us free.

I remember and wonder why?
In fall, in summer; times we had
Will be no more. Journeys have
Their end.
I remember and wonder why?

In the sacred suffering of lung
Spine and groin,
You cease, fly away

To what? To autumn, to
Winter, to brown leaves, to
Wind where no lark sings; yet
Through dominion of air, jaw and fire

I remember!

Eric Dolphy, you swung
A beautiful axe. You lived a clean
Life. You were young
Then
You
Died.

Mellowness & Flight
For Charlie Parker

GEORGE BARLOW

ever heard Bird
flap his wings

ever heard him
play Lover Man
Laura
Just Friends

ever taken
his mellowness in
& felt

like
you were
flying
with him

shining like him

a bright blackbird
slicing blue sky

sweetly & freely

ever heard Bird
flap his wings

Yardbird's Skull
For Charlie Parker

OWEN DODSON

The bird is lost,
Dead, with all the music:
Whole sunsets heard the brain's music
Faded to last horizon notes.
I do not know why I hold
This skull, smaller than a walnut's,
Against my ear,
Expecting to hear
The smashed fear
Of childhood from . . . bone;
Expecting to see
Wind nosing red and purple,
Strange gold and magic
On bubbled windowpanes
Of childhood. Shall I hear?
I should hear: this skull
Has been with violets
Not Yorick, or the gravedigger,
Yapping his yelling story,
This skull has been in air,
Sensed his brother, the swallow,
(Its talent for snow and crumbs).
Flown to lost Atlantis islands,
Places of dreaming, swimming, lemmings.
O I shall hear skull skull,
Hear your lame music,
Believe music rejects undertaking,
Limps back.
Remember tiny lasting, we get lonely:
Come sing, come sing, come sing sing
And sing.

john coltrane
an impartial review

A. B. SPELLMAN

may he have new life like the fall
fallen tree, wet moist rotten enough
to see shoots stalks branches & green
leaves (& may the roots) grow into his side.

around the back of the mind, in its closet
is a string, i think, a coil around things.
listen to *summertime*, think of spring, negroes
cats in the closet, anything that makes a rock

of your eye. imagine you steal. you are frightened
you want help. you are sorry you are born with ears.

After the Rain

STANLEY CROUCH

John's words were the words
Bird and the other winged creatures
sang:
     How the darkness could
     and would someday
     sink behind the sun,
     how we, when we grew
     to ourselves, past what we were,
     how we would dance outside
     bucking the eyes of all stars and all light
     how we would be as gentle
     as the rebuilt wings of a broken sparrow,
     how we would lick back the rain

and wash ourselves with light
and our eyes would meet His
our God, our Om, our Allah, our Brahman.
And we, like all oceans,
would know
and love each other.
Salaam.

Sopranosound, Memory of John

SHARON BOURKE

Soft
The stars are melting,
Smooth becomes the night
Around his shoulders.

Like two coins resting on his eyelids
Is the light,
And sound now, utterly,
He stays.

Listen to the reed,

To his mind
As it opens and closes the valves of the universe,

To his breath
Softly, smoothly spiraling,

To his song
From the throat of future time,

Listen
To John.

Here Where Coltrane Is

MICHAEL S. HARPER

Soul and race
are private dominions,
memories and modal
songs, a tenor blossoming,
which would paint suffering
a clear color but is not in
this Victorian house
without oil in zero degree
weather and a forty-mile-an-hour wind;
it is all a well-knit family:
a *love supreme.*
Oak leaves pile up on walkway
and steps, catholic as apples
in a special mist of clear white
children who love my children.
I play "Alabama"
on a warped record player
skipping the scratches
on your faces over the fibrous
conical hairs of plastic
under the wooden floors.

Dreaming on a train from New York
to Philly, you hand out six
notes which become an anthem
to our memories of you:
oak, birch, maple,
apple, cocoa, rubber.
For this reason Martin is dead;
for this reason Malcolm is dead;
for this reason Coltrane is dead;
in the eyes of my first son are the browns
of these men and their music.

For Malcolm Who Walks
    in the Eyes of Our Children

Malcolm

LUCILLE CLIFTON

nobody mentioned war
but doors were closed
black women shaved their heads
black men rustled in the alleys like leaves
prophets were ambushed as they spoke
and from their holes black eagles flew
screaming through the streets

Portrait of Malcolm X
For Charles Baker

ETHERIDGE KNIGHT

He has the sign
of the time shining
in his eyes   the high sign

His throat moans
Moses on Sinai and cracks
stones

His lips lay full and flowered
by the breast of Mother Africa

His forehead is red
and sacrosanct and
smooth as time and
love for you

Malcolm X

For Dudley Randall

GWENDOLYN BROOKS

Original.
Ragged-round.
Rich-robust.

He had the hawk-man's eyes.
We gasped. We saw the maleness.
The maleness raking out and making guttural the air
and pushing us to walls.

And in a soft and fundamental hour
a sorcery devout and vertical
beguiled the world.

He opened us—
who was a key,

who was a man.

For Malcolm X

MARGARET WALKER

All you violated ones with gentle hearts;
You violent dreamers whose cries shout heartbreak;
Whose voices echo clamors of our cool capers,
And whose black faces have hollowed pits for eyes.
All you gambling sons and hooked children and bowery
        bums
Hating white devils and black bourgeoisie,
Thumbing your noses at your burning red suns,
Gather round this coffin and mourn your dying swan.

Snow-white moslem head-dress around a dead black face!
Beautiful were your sand-papering words against our skins!
Our blood and water pour from your flowing wounds.
You have cut open our breasts and dug scalpels in our
    brains.
When and Where will another come to take your holy
    place?
Old man mumbling in his dotage, or crying child, unborn?

Aardvark

JULIA FIELDS

Since
    Malcolm died
    That old aardvark
    has got a sort of fame
    for himself—
    I mean, of late, when I read
    The dictionary the first
    Thing I see
    Is that animal staring at me.
And then
    I think of Malcom—
    How he read
    in the prisons
    And on the planes
    And everywhere
    And how he wrote
    About old Aardvark.
Looks like Malcom X helped
Bring attention to a lot of things
We never thought about before.

i remember . . .

MAE JACKSON

i remember . . .
january,
1968
it's snow,
the desire that i had to build
a black snowman
and place him upon
Malcolm's grave.

    8/15/68

Malcolm, a Thousandth Poem

CONRAD KENT RIVERS

When brothers build a city
Down in valleys
And through mountains,
Across plains slashed by winds
Forever African;

Your flame fires them on.
Black men and white men discovering
Dialogue.

Death is fit for a monkey's laughter,
Useless. Immortality comes by
Breaking laws.

Let my women mourn for you.
Your articulation is a silent, Amen.

For Malcolm: After Mecca
My whole life has been a chronology of — *changes.*

GERALD W. BARRAX

You lie now in many coffins
in parlors where your name
is dropped more heavily even than Death
sent you crashing to the stage
on which you had exorcised our shame.

In little rooms they gather now
bringing their own memories of your pilgrimage
they come and go
speaking of revolution
without knowing as you learned
how static hate is
without recognizing the man you were
lay in our shame
and your growth into martyrdom.

El-Hajj Malik El-Shabazz (Malcolm X)
O masks and metamorphoses of Ahab, Native Son

ROBERT HAYDEN

I

The icy evil that struck his father down
and ravished his mother into madness
trapped him in violence of a punished self
struggling to break free.

As Home Boy, as Dee-troit Red,
he fled his name, became the quarry of
his own obsessed pursuit.

He conked his hair and Lindy-hopped,
zoot-suited jiver, swinging those chicks
in the hot rose and reefer glow.

His injured childhood bullied him.
He skirmished in the Upas trees
and cannibal flowers of the American Dream —

but could not hurt the enemy
powered against him there.

II

Sometimes the dark that gave his life
its cold satanic sheen would shift
a little, and he saw himself
floodlit and eloquent;

yet how could he, "Satan" in The Hole,
guess what the waking dream foretold?

Then false dawn of vision came;
he fell upon his face before
a racist Allah pledged to wrest him from
the hellward-thrusting hands of Calvin's Christ —

to free him and his kind
from Yakub's white-faced treachery.
He rose redeemed from all but prideful anger,

though adulterate attars could not cleanse
him of the odors of the pit.

III

Asalam alaikum!

He X'd his name, became his people's anger,
exhorted them to vengeance for their past;
rebuked, admonished them,

their scourger who
would shame them, drive them from
the lush ice gardens of their servitude.

Asalam alaikum!

Rejecting Ahab, he was of Ahab's tribe.
"Strike through the mask!"

IV

Time. "The martyr's time," he said.
Time and the karate killer,
knifer, gunman. Time that brought
ironic trophies as his faith

twined sparking round the bole,
the fruit of neo-Islam.
"The martyr's time."

But first, the ebb time pilgrimage
toward revelation, hejira to
his final metamorphosis;

Labbayk! Labbayk!

He fell upon his face before
Allah the raceless in whose blazing Oneness all
were one. He rose renewed renamed, became
much more than there was time for him to be.

For Malcolm Who Walks
in the Eyes of Our Children
QUINCY TROUPE

He had been coming a very long time,
had been here many times before
in the flesh of other persons
in the spirit of other gods

His eyes had seen flesh turned too stone,
had seen stone turned too flesh
had swam within the minds
of a billion great heroes,

had walked amongst builders
of nations, of the Sphinx, had built
with his own hands those nations,

had come flying across time a cosmic spirit,
an idea, a thought wave transcending
flesh fusion spirit of all centuries,
had come soaring like a sky break

above ominous clouds of sulphur
in a stride so enormous it spanned
the breadth of a peoples bloodshed,

came singing like Coltrane breathing life
into stone statues formed from lies

Malcolm, flaming cosmic spirit who walks
amongst us, we hear your voice
speaking wisdom in the wind,
we see your vision in the life/fires of men,
in our incredible young children
who watch your image
flaming in the sun

A Poem for Heroes

A Poem for Heroes

JULIA FIELDS

Blood will not serve—
The grass will find its way.

Flesh will not serve—
The dead live in the living
And there will always be someone.

Time will not serve.
The dust of the valiant
Will put out the eyes
Will clog the lungs—
How shall we keep
The brave without heirs?
The wind will find its way.

Tell the vigilantes
With the sheets and shells
Blood cannot serve;
Tell the little ones.
Tell the hordes of armies
Navies, generals and
Other functionaries,
Blood cannot serve.
Wars will not serve.
There are always
Heirs to heroism
It is in the nature of the world.
It cannot be obstructed.
There will always be someone,

Some hero drawing strength,
Drawing endurance from
Old bones mouldering
And rivulets of plasma

Grown into the acquiescent ground
By rain, by dews
From fragrances of flowers.
Blood will not serve.

from: Words in the Mourning Time
ROBERT HAYDEN

I

For King, for Robert Kennedy,
destroyed by those they could not save,
for King for Kennedy I mourn.
And for America, self-destructive, self-betrayed.

I grieve. Yet know the vanity
of grief—through power of
The Blessed Exile's
transilluminating word

aware of how these deaths, how all
the agonies of our deathbed childbed age
are process, major means whereby,
oh dreadfully, our humanness must be achieved.

Dory Miller
(black man who earned a purple heart at Pearl Harbor)
SAM CORNISH

he left the kitchen
long enough to earn a purple
heart

downed three planes before
the death
of his ship

when he died
four yellow dead men
on his hands

he was still peeling potatoes
his medal somewhere in the pages
of a book

Emmett Till

JAMES A. EMANUEL

I hear a whistling
Through the water.
Little Emmett
Won't be still.
He keeps floating
Round the darkness,
Edging through
The silent chill.

Tell me, please,
That bedtime story
Of the fairy
River Boy
Who swims forever,
Deep in treasures,
Necklaced in
A coral toy.

The Last Quatrain of the Ballad of Emmett Till

GWENDOLYN BROOKS

after the murder,
after the burial

Emmett's mother is a pretty-faced thing;
the tint of pulled taffy.
She sits in a red room,
drinking black coffee.
She kisses her killed boy.
And she is sorry.
Chaos in windy grays
through a red prairie.

Montgomery

For Rosa Parks

SAM CORNISH

white woman have you heard
she is too tired to sit in the back
her feet are two hundred years old

move to the back or walk
around to the side door how
long can a woman be a cow

your feet will not move
and you never listen
but even if it rains empty

seats will ride through town
i walk for my children
my feet two hundred years old

Street Demonstration

"Hurry up Lucille or we won't get arrested with our group."
— an eight-year-old demonstrator, 1963

MARGARET WALKER

We're hoping to be arrested
And hoping to go to jail
We'll sing and shout and pray
For Freedom and for Justice
And for Human Dignity
The fighting may be long
And some of us will die
But Liberty is costly
And ROME they say to me
Was not built in one day.

Hurry up, Lucille, Hurry up
We're Going to Miss Our Chance to go to Jail.

Girl Held Without Bail

"In an unjust state the only place for a just man is in jail."

MARGARET WALKER

I like it here just fine
And I don't want no bail

My sister's here
My mother's here
And all my girl friends too.
I want my rights
I'm fighting for my rights

I want to be treated
Just like *anybody* else
I want to be treated
Just like *everybody* else

*I like it fine in Jail
And I don't want no Bail.*

Birmingham 1963

RAYMOND R. PATTERSON

Sunday morning and her mother's hands
Weaving the two thick braids of her springing hair,
Pulling her sharply by one bell-rope when she would
Not sit still, setting her ringing,
While the radio church choir prophesied the hour
With theme and commercials, while the whole house tingled;
And she could not stand still in that awkward air;
Her dark face shining, her mother now moving the tiny buttons,
Blue against blue, the dress which took all night making,
That refused to stay fastened;
There was some pull which hurried her out to Sunday School
Toward the lesson and the parable's good news,
The quiet escape from the warring country of her feelings,
The confused landscape of grave issues and people.

But now we see
Now we see through the glass of her mother's wide screaming
Eyes into the room where the homemade bomb

Blew the room down where her daughter had gone:
Under the leaves of hymnals, the plaster and stone,
The blue dress, all undone —
The day undone to the bone —
Her still, dull face, her quiet hair;
Alone amid the rubble, amid the people
Who perish, being innocent.

Martin Luther King Jr.

GWENDOLYN BROOKS

A man went forth with gifts.

He was a prose poem.
He was a tragic grace.
He was a warm music.

He tried to heal the vivid volcanoes.
His ashes are
     reading the world.

His Dream still wishes to anoint
     the barricades of faith and of control.

His word still burns the center of the sun,
     above the thousands and the
     hundred thousands.

The word was Justice. It was spoken.

So it shall be spoken.
So it shall be done.

Rites of Passage
To MLK Jr.

AUDRE LORDE

Now rock the boat to a fare-thee-well.
Once we suffered dreaming
into the place where the children are playing
their child's games
where the children are hoping
knowledge survives
if unknowing
they follow the game
without winning.

Their fathers are dying
back to the freedom of wise children playing
at knowing
their fathers are dying
whose deaths will not free them
of growing from knowledge
of knowing
when the game becomes foolish
a dangerous pleading
for time out of power.

Quick
children kiss us
we are growing through dream.

Death of Dr. King

SAM CORNISH

#1

we sit outside
the bars   the dime stores
everything is closed today

we are mourning
our hands filled with bricks
a brother is dead

my eyes are white and cold
water is in my hands

this is grief

#2

after the water
the broken bread
we return
to our separate
places

in our heads
bodies collapse
and grow again

the city boils
black men
jump out of trees

King Lives

JILL WITHERSPOON BOYER

King still lives
in some crowded bar
waiting to be knifed over 50¢
that he doesn't have anyway
He does not know
to use the hands
his children strain to catch —
for fists
His is not a boxer's heart
But then Gandhi promised nothing
except how it feels
to be out there alone

Outside the bar
bloody sirens
crowd murmuring popeyes
for the last look

Martin's Blues

MICHAEL S. HARPER

He came apart in the open,
the slow motion cameras
falling quickly
neither alive nor kicking;
stone blind dead
on the balcony
that old melody
etched his black lips

in a pruned echo:
We shall overcome
some day —
Yes we did!
Yes we did!

Langston Blues

DUDLEY RANDALL

Your lips were so laughing
Langston man
your lips were so singing
minstrel man
how death could touch them
hard to understand

Your lips that laughed
and sang so well
your lips that brought
laughter from hell
are silent now
no more to tell

So let us sing
a Langston blues
sing a lost
Langston blues
long gone song
for Langston Hughes

Do Nothing till You Hear from Me

For Langston Hughes

DAVID HENDERSON

i arrive   /Langston
the new york times told me when to come
but i attended your funeral
late
by habit of colored folk
and didnt miss a thing

you lie on saint nicholas avenue
between the black ghetto & sugar hill
where slick black limousines await yr body
for the final haul
from neutral santa claus avenue
harlem usa

you are dressed sharp & dark as death
yr cowlick is smooth
like the negro gentleman
in the ebony whiskey ads/
gone is yr puff of face
yr paunch of chest
tho yr lips are fuller now
especially
on the side
where hazard had you
                a cigarette/

two sisters
          felines of egypt
vigil yr dead body
one is dressed in a bean picker's brown
the other is an erstwhile gown
of the harlem renaissance/
they chatter

like all the sapphires
of Kingfish's harem/
                    old sisters
                              old relations

in writing the fine details
of yr last production
you would have the black sapphires/   there
guardians of yr coffin
                    yr argosy
                        in life & death
the last time blues/
                    with no hesitations . . .

                [day of the vernal winds/1967]

For All Things Black and Beautiful
For Langston Hughes

CONRAD KENT RIVERS

For all things black and beautiful,
The brown faces you loved so well and long,
the endless roads leading back to Harlem.
  For all things black and beautiful
  The seeking and the labor always waiting and coming
  Until you began to dream of Nubian queens
  And black kings shifting the dust of eternity
  Before the white man brought his shame and God.

    For all things black and beautiful
    It took a lot of stones from little white boys
    To produce the poem and quench the first desire to taste
    Their nectar and the black wine of black empires
    Flowing through your black bursting bewildered body.

For all things black and beautiful
And your Indian grandmother weaving tragic tales
Until the sea consumed you and the world you had loved
In ports and places few of your black brothers knew.

For all things black and beautiful
And the strange house in Taos and your white old man
Under a yellow Mexican sun dying black and moaning
Those weary blues until you came home to Harlem seeking
A way and worship and luster in the jive and the jazz
Once chained to the bottom of slave ships and whipped
In the public squares of our most democratic colorful cities.

For all things black and beautiful
The white savior and the black Christ dreaming dreams
While a black brother hangs from an oak without branches.

For all things black and beautiful
And big black Bessie doing her solo thrice times
Until Louie saves her by blasting his golden horn
And the whites shout and the blacks dance and night cries
Coming with her bullets in our bodies and death in our
        brains
But we cry out and finance our misery until our guts
Belong to the holy holy company and they laugh and eat well
While we die young and strong though tired of time
        payments.

For all things black and beautiful
Your poetry's a monument to our violated homes without
        hope
As we go weeping behind your box wanting to hear your
        tunes.
But if our poet is dead and Simple no longer sips divinity
Then we have not heard it in the breeze that blows our
        music
And our song into the vespers and the dens of white
        America

When our very faces are not wanted somehow we do exist
	there.

For all things black and beautiful
The music you heard in the hallways and hid in the noun
The street woman you loved and saved with a sober ballad
The urban holocaust that swept you through the ghetto-
	ghetto land
The barbeque and sweet potatoes too many nights you went
	without
The sounds you heard in your head like dripping meal from
	cornbread
The dishwater like blood on your hands and filth on your
	heart
The Renaissance and Du Bois and Robeson and Carl and
	Arna and Zora
All gone like a Russian moon passes through the bight of
	Benin.

For all things black and beautiful
And Mali rising again and Timbuktu spreading culture
	across the land
And Yardbird smoking and cleansing this roomy world of
	dry ashes
Until Sweet Sue understands the beauty of her black sunset
	silk skin
And the glory of her carmelite brown brighter than a blue
	red sun
Echoing the ancient truths of her own black culture and
	being.

For all things black and beautiful seen through your eyes:
Willie Mays doing his ballet in centerfield and Lady Day
	praying
And Harlem The Black Mother weeping and my own wet
	eyes, Langston
Feeling the darkness and the decline of the kingdom and
	glory of all

Things you made so black and beautiful in your fashion and
  way.
Africa is in your grave and may all the elements find peace
  with you.

Langston

MARI EVANS

standing on 127th the
smell of collards
the sound
of cueballs and the
Primitive Church
of The Universal God he
told it like it
was . . .

Lumumba's Grave

LANGSTON HUGHES

Lumumba was black
And he didn't trust
The whores all powdered
With uranium dust.

Lumumba was black
And he didn't believe
The lies thieves shook
Through their "freedom" sieve.

Lumumba was black.
His blood was red—
And for being a man
They killed him dead.

They buried Lumumba
In an unmarked grave.
But he needs no marker—
For air is his grave.

Sun is his grave,
Moon is, stars are,
Space is his grave.

tomorrow the heroes

A. B. SPELLMAN

tomorrow the heroes
will be named willie. their
hair will be the bushes that grow
everywhere the beast walks. america

is white. america is not. white
is not the slow kerneling of seed
in earth like the willies, the grass
the roots that grapple the beast

in the swamps. the williecong are earth
walking. ile-ife succor the williecong.
there is no other hope.

If We Cannot Live as People

If we cannot live as people, we will at least try to die like men

— an Attica inmate

CHARLES LYNCH

Inspire our sons to seek their man-shadows
gauntleted, spread-eagled, mired in blood
seeping beneath walls six-feet deep
where Attica attacked no Attucks,
but nobly raging brothers
white-washed chronicles shall give
no plaque, no wreath,

no amnesty for truth massacred
by orderlies of law slinking
along the parapets of hate,
goose-stepping to shatter flesh gasping
at the gate of non-negotiable slaughter.

Black death will not be defined by murder
(ignoble beast that charged through war-zone D).
Illicit blood sanctifies life again, again again again:
generations of Sharpeville, Orangeburg, Attica,
reckoning peoplehood,
shadowing the shadow-men.

H. Rap Brown

HENRY BLAKELY

America will never forgive you,
H. Rap Brown,
for making her Nigras mean.

to Bobby Seale
LUCILLE CLIFTON

feel free.
like my daddy
always said
jail wasn't made
for dogs,
was made for
men

Ali
LLOYD CORBIN (DJANGATOLUM)

Ali
Is our prince
Regal and Black
A glass that could fall
but never break
A flower without rain
that never could die
Ali
Is our prince

Paul Robeson

GWENDOLYN BROOKS

That time
we all heard it,
cool and clear,
cutting across the hot grit of the day.
The major Voice.
The adult Voice
forgoing Rolling River,
forgoing tearful tale of bale and barge
and other symptoms of an old despond.
Warning, in music-words
devout and large,
that we are each other's
harvest:
we are each other's
business:
we are each other's
magnitude and bond.

The Music
After Reading *All God's Dangers: The Life of Nate Shaw*

EVERETT HOAGLAND

Your archival voice,
our long blues song,
life's story
coughed up
the blood soaked cotton

gag. Blue blood
blues.

Book-long,
blue steel guitar blues.

Your Smith and Wesson
.32 gun metal voice.
Six strings.

*What did they call you
when you didn't yield?*

> "If you were a :
> white man : principled
> mule : stubborn
> nigger : *Crazy*"

You were a blue steel guitar

and your wife was
a fiddle and a tambourine.
Hannah. Soft as cotton
and as strong.

And your wife was
a fiddle and a tambourine,
and we your sons are
banjos,
and we your daughters
cane fifes

playing your gun metal voice,

playing your blue steel
guitar book-long song
crazy!

Who Shined Shoes in Times Square
LANCE JEFFERS

Who shined shoes in Times Square,
his belly is the richest seedbed for human corn:
Speech stamped slowly through his teeth,
   his red eyes hooded sighs of death,
serenity swam acres of lake in his brain,
an Indian girl combed a runaway's wool in the
dimmest corner of his soul:

His acceptance was woven to my flesh like sk .

"Jeff, we been sleeping on spikes so long
that cement feel good."

Through his loving candid gaze
I see a nation fall:

Through the majesty of his
melody, I see a nation rise . . .

Eulogy for Alvin Frost
AUDRE LORDE

I.

Black men bleeding to death inside themselves
inside their fine strong bodies
inside their stomachs
inside their heads
a hole
as large as a dum-dum bullet
eaten away from the inside
dead at 37.

Windows are holes made to let in the light
in Newark airport at dawn I read
of your death by illumination
I walk through February dawn in Newark airport
and the carpets are dark and the windows are smoky
to keep out the coming sun
I plummet down through a hole in the carpet
seeking immediate ground for my feet to remember
to embrace
my wild toes have no wisdom
no strength to resist
they curl in a passion of grief
of fury uprooted
It is dawn in the airport and nothing is open?
I cannot even plant you a tree
because the earth is still frozen
I write a card to say
that machines grew the flowers I send
to throw into your grave.

On occasion we passed in the hallway
usually silent and hurried but fighting
on the same side.
You congratulate me on my last book
in a Black Caucus meeting
you are distinguished
by your genuine laughter
and you might have been that long lost
second grade seat-mate named Alvin
grown into some other magic
but we never had time
enough
to talk.

II.

In an airplane heading south
the earth grows slowly greener

we pass over a swimming pool
filled with blue water
and this winter is almost over
I don't want to write a natural poem
I want to write about the unnatural death
of a young man at 37
eating himself for courage in secret
until he died
bleeding to death inside.
He will be eulogized in echoes
by a ghost of those winters
that haunt all morning people
wearing away our days like smiling water
in southern pools
leaving psychic graffiti
to clog the walls of our hearts
to carve out ulcers within our stomachs
from which we explode
or bleed to death.

III.

I am tired of writing memorial poems to Black men
who I was on the brink of knowing
I am weary like fig trees
weighted like a crepe myrtle
With all the black substance poured into earth
before earth is ready to bear.

I am tired of holy deaths
of the ulcerous illuminations the cerebral accidents
the psychology of the oppressed.
Psychology is the study of mental events
manslaughter of the mindless
defining mental health as the ability
to repress
knowledge of the world's cruelty.

The day after your burial
John Wade slid off his chair
onto the carpet in the student cafeteria
between Abnormal Psychology and a half finished
cup of black coffee
and died there on the floor
of a cerebral accident
between Abnormal and coffee
blue cafeteria guards hustled him out
by the back door between classes
and we never knew until last week
that he'd even been ill.

IV.

Dear Danny who does not know me
I am
writing to you for your father
whom I barely knew
except at meetings where he was distinguished
by his genuine laughter
and his kind bright words
Please cry
whenever it hurts
and remember to laugh
even when you do battle
stay away from coffee and fried plastic
even when it looks like chicken
and grow up
black and strong and beautiful
but not too soon.

We need you
and there are so few
left.

Shade

Transformation

QUINCY TROUPE

catch the blues song
of wind in your bleeding
black hand, wrap it around
your strong gnarled fingers
then turn it into a soft-nosed pen
and sit down, and write
the love poem of your life.

We Dance like Ella Riffs

CAROLYN M. RODGERS

the room was a
red glow, there was
a warm close pulsating.
Chairs and tables were
                    sprawled like a semi-circle
bowing to the band stand where
                    ripples of light lingered
on the silver tracings of player's
soulpieces and
brightened and glistened and
dazzjangled
like tear drops
in a corner
          suspended
and spit on by the light

again and again and oooooh

splu dah dee
do dah'um dah
spleeeeee

the dancers were
soft breezes, smooth
jerky moving
ballooon move the air
no moving was the
wrong moving
roll with the notes
sift through the beats
pause, the music
                    sure carelessly careful, caresses cor-recting the air
we are music
sound & motion imitate us
each of us,
Black variations
                    on a
Round theme
any one
of us —
an infinite, essential note
                    sounding down this world.

Coal

AUDRE LORDE

I

Is the total black, being spoken
From the earth's inside.
There are many kinds of open.

How a diamond comes into a knot of flame
How a sound comes into a word, coloured
By who pays what for speaking.

Some words are open
Like a diamond on glass windows
Singing out within the crash of passing sun
Then there are words like stapled wagers
In a perforated book — buy and sign and tear apart —
And come whatever wills all chances
The stub remains
An ill-pulled tooth with a ragged edge.
Some words live in my throat
Breeding like adders. Others know sun
Seeking like gypsies over my tongue
To explode through my lips
Like young sparrows bursting from shell.
Some words
Bedevil me.

Love is a word another kind of open —
As a diamond comes into a knot of flame
I am black because I come from the earth's inside
Take my word for jewel in your open light.

Naturally

AUDRE LORDE

Since Naturally Black is Naturally Beautiful
I must be proud
and, naturally,
Black and
Beautiful
who always was a trifle

yellow
and plain
though proud
before.

So I've given up pomades
having spent the summer sunning
and feeling
naturally
free
(and if I die of skin
   cancer
   oh well — one less
   black and beautiful me)
For no agency spends millions
to prevent my summer's tanning
and nobody trembles nightly
with a fear
of lily cities being swallowed
by a summer ocean
of naturally woolly hair.

But I've bought my can of
Natural Hair Spray —
made and marketed in Watts —
still thinking more
Proud Beautiful Black Women
could better make and use
Black bread.

Rib Sandwich

WILLIAM J. HARRIS

I wanted a rib sandwich

So I got into my car
and drove as fast as I could
to a little black restaurant-
bar
and walked in
and so doing
walked out
of
America

and didn't even
need a passport

Determination

JOHN HENRIK CLARKE

My feet have felt the sands
Of many nations,
I have drunk the water
Of many springs,
I am old,
Older than the Pyramids,
I am older than the race
That oppresses me,
I will live on . . .
I will outlive oppression,
I will outlive oppressors.

Oppression

LANGSTON HUGHES

Now dreams
Are not available
To the dreamers,
Nor songs
To the singers.

In some lands
Dark night
And cold steel
Prevail—
But the dream
Will come back,
And the song
Break
Its jail.

A Different Image

DUDLEY RANDALL

The age
requires this task:
create
a different image;
re-animate
the mask.

Shatter the icons of slavery and fear.
Replace
the leer
of the minstrel's burnt-cork face

with a proud, serene
and classic bronze of Benin.

Roses and Revolutions

DUDLEY RANDALL

Musing on roses and revolutions,
I saw night close down on the earth like a great dark wing,
and the lighted cities were like tapers in the night,
and I heard the lamentations of a million hearts
regretting life and crying for the grave,
and I saw the Negro lying in the swamp with his face
    blown off,
and in northern cities with his manhood maligned and felt
    the writhing
of his viscera like that of the hare hunted down or the bear
    at bay,
and I saw men working and taking no joy in their work
and embracing the hard-eyed whore with joyless excitement
and lying with wives and virgins in impotence.

And as I groped in darkness
and felt the pain of millions,
gradually, like day driving night across the continent,
I saw dawn upon them like the sun a vision
of a time when all men walk proudly through the earth
and the bombs and missiles lie at the bottom of the ocean
like the bones of dinosaurs buried under the shale of eras,
and men strive with each other not for power or the
    accumulation of paper
but in joy create for others the house, the poem, the game
    of athletic beauty.

Then washed in the brightness of this vision,
I saw how in its radiance would grow and be nourished
    and suddenly
burst into terrible and splendid bloom
the blood-red flower of revolution.

Revolutionary Dreams

NIKKI GIOVANNI

i used to dream militant
dreams of taking
over america to show
these white folks how it should be
done
i used to dream radical dreams
of blowing everyone away with my perceptive powers
of correct analysis
i even used to think i'd be the one
to stop the riot and negotiate the peace
then i awoke and dug
that if i dreamed natural
dreams of being a natural
woman doing what a woman
does when she's natural
i would have a revolution

Dreams

NIKKI GIOVANNI

in my younger years
before i learned
black people aren't
suppose to dream
i wanted to be
a raelet
and say "dr o wn d in my youn tears"
or "tal kin bout tal kin bout"
or marjorie hendricks and grind
all up against the mic
and scream
"baaaaaby nightandday
baaaaaby nightandday"
then as i grew and matured
i became more sensible
and decided i would
settle down
and just become
a sweet inspiration

God Send Easter

LUCILLE CLIFTON

and we will lace the
jungle on
and step out
brilliant as birds
against the concrete country
feathers waving as we

dance toward jesus
sun reflecting mango
and apple as we
glory in our skin

Who Can Be Born Black

MARI EVANS

Who
can be born black
and not   '
sing
the wonder of it
the joy
the
challenge

Who
can be born
black
and not exult!

I Am a Black Woman

MARI EVANS

I am a black woman
the music of my song
some sweet arpeggio of tears
is written in a minor key
and I
can be heard humming in the night

Can be heard
         humming
in the night

I saw my mate leap screaming to the sea
and I/with these hands/cupped the lifebreath
from my issue in the canebrake
I lost Nat's swinging body in a rain of tears
and heard my son scream all the way from Anzio
for Peace he never knew. . . . I
learned Da Nang and Pork Chop Hill
in anguish
Now my nostrils know the gas
and these trigger tire/d fingers
seek the softness in my warrior's beard

I
am a black woman
tall as a cypress
strong
beyond all definition still
defying place
and time
and circumstance
   assailed
      impervious
          indestructible
Look
  on me and be
renewed

The Way It Is

GLORIA ODEN

I have always known
that had I been blonde
blue-eyed
with skin fabled white as the unicorn's
with cheeks tinted and pearled
as May morning on the lips of a rose
such commercial virtues
could never have led me to assume myself
anywhere near as beautiful as
my mother
whose willow fall of black hair
—now pirate silver—
I brushed as a child
(earning five cents)
when shaken free from the bun
as wrapped round and pinned
it billowed in a fine mist
from her proud shoulders
to her waist.

Brown as I am, she is browner.
Walnut
like the satin leaves of the oak
that fallen overwinter in woods
where night comes quickly
and whose wind-peaked piles
deepen the shadows of
such seizure.

Moreover, she is tall.
At her side standing
I feel I am still
that scarecrow child of
yesteryear:

owl-eyed
toothed, boned, and angled
opposite to her
soft southern presence —
an inaudible allegiance
but sweetening her attendance
upon strangers and friends.

Dark hair, dark skin
these are the dominant measures of
my sense of beauty
which explains possibly
why being a black girl
in a country of white strangers
I am so pleased with myself.

Chromo

SARAH WEBSTER FABIO

Color it
blue funk
this sound
that tears
singing
from me
in beauty
of agony;
this colored
thing —

so many
blues,

the hues
of my
spent days:
blue, the eyes
of my soul
starred
in twilight
gaze.

Color —
in high
tones, low —
this non-
harmonic
sound
full of woe
"me"
chromo. . .
chromo. . .
chromo. . .

Negritude

JAMES A. EMANUEL

Black is the first nail I ever stepped on;
Black the hand that dried my tears.
Black is the first old man I ever noticed;
Black the burden of his years.

Black is waiting in the darkness;
Black the ground where hoods have lain.
Black is the sorrow-misted story;
Black the brotherhood of pain.

Black is a quiet iron door;
Black the path that leads behind.
Black is a detour through the years;
Black the diary of the mind.

Black is Gabriel Prosser's knuckles;
Black Sojourner's naked breast.
Black is a schoolgirl's breathless mother;
Black her child who led the rest.

Black is the purring of a motor;
Black the foot when the light turns green.
Black is last year's dusty paper;
Black the headlines yet unseen.

Black is a burden bravely chanted:
Black cross of sweat for a nation's rise.
Black is a boy who knows his heroes;
Black the way a hero dies.

A Poem About Beauty, Blackness, Poetry (and how to be all three)

LINDA BROWN BRAGG

"Black folks have got to be superhuman,"
    I said to the earnest young
    revolutionary beautiful Black sister.

And she said, "don't tell me
I oughta be lookin' for beauty
when I have ta fight these honkies
every minute I am breathin'."

And I said "right—why you think
Aretha, Baraka, Roberta
move us the way that they cer-tain-ly do?

And why you think your grandmother
had so many green plants around
in her itty-bitty creaky-floored house
that she couldn't quite get clean
no matter how hard she tried?

And why you think we had to wear those Sunday dresses
that had to be starched and flat-ironed
no matter how late it was on Saturday night?

Because we have always been super-human,"
I said, believing in beauty,
"so now we got to be super (revolutionary
beautiful and Black) human."

And she nodded, the weight of it all too heavy
for her spare shoulders, and went
back to her revolutionary reading,

While I sat there thinking how
young woman bones of Black strength
have always been
poems for our people.

Our Blackness Did Not Come to Us Whole

LINDA BROWN BRAGG

Our blackness did not come to us whole
    (we who are older)
but in bits of burnt orange and
pungent brown.
It seeped through the white gloves,
the Sunday meeting manner.

It crept up the hem of our dresses,
staining.

Our discomfort showed.

We twitched and twisted, trying to
hide the creeping afro
that peeked from beneath our pink cherried hats,
hair going back, back, back,
(we all really knew to where).

And so we gradually turned black and
had *our* mothers also to contend with . . .
"But ten years ago you marched for mixing in,"
she said. "I told you then it didn't make
no sense. And now you're telling me
my flag should be

> red
> black
> and
> green.

And who ever heard of a *third* world anyway?
I'm worn out just tryin' to make it in the
first one the Lord give me."

So, darkened by the spreading word,
we learned to be comfortable
with color

and somebody told us that it was alright to be
middle-aged and "militant,"
that the movement would accept all
who had been permanently dyed
as long as we had not

> permanently died.

10/16/73

When the Wine Was Gone

ALVIN AUBERT

we lived in language all our black selves,
wordsound was our food. was what we got
high on when the wine was gone. was all
the world we had to move around in. was
the blues once we slipped past steal away
to jesus to get a hold of his old man's throat
dam his breath to form again that one big long
last word freedom. was ragtime then jazz
was all the rap boogie to bop that kept
charlie dancing till we could figure out how
he rocked. try his rock on. find it didn't
fit. make a rock of our own to the rhythm
of a painful black movement in the mind
that springs you have to move with when it
spring or break and die. break, brother,
sister, and die.

Cold Term

AMIRI BARAKA (LEROI JONES)

All the things. The objects.
Cold freeze of the park, while
passing. People there. White inside
outside on horses trotting ignorantly
There is so much pain for our blackness
so much beauty there, if we think to what
our beautiful selves would make
of the world, steaming turning blackouts
over cold georgia, the spirits hover

waiting for the world to arrive at ecstasy.
Why cant we love each other and be beautiful?
Why do the beautiful corner each other and spit
poison? Why do the beautiful not hangout together
and learn to do away with evil? Why are the beautiful
not living together and feeling each other's trials?
Why are the beautiful not walking with their arms around
each other laughing softly at the soft laughter of black
      beauty?
Why are the beautiful dreading each other, and hiding from
each other? Why are the beautiful sick and divided
like myself?

Shade
For Gayle

CHARLES LYNCH

Baby, depend upon it:
Somehow everything beneath the sun
inhabits inhibition to a fault:

yellow tulips   smile   in the air   (you walk)
   but fade   down in the mouth
of the Mason jar   on your window sill:

As earthward   my face   peeling
grafted reflections   from memory's flowering mirror:

"he have . . . gray-green eyes . . .
sorta light-skin . . . real keen features . . ."

"high yella . . . redbone"

"but what happen to your hair?":

Phrases surplused from the hour
real words unclenched their jaws:

Now whatever shade I am   or seek
let light inviolable   be my black focus,

not the hocus complexion
in my brooding blood:

We reach out   touch
                          All love

For Each of You

For Each of You

AUDRE LORDE

Be who you are and will be
learn to cherish
that boisterous Black Angel that drives you
up one day and down another
protecting the place where your power rises
running like hot blood
from the same source
as your pain.

When you are hungry
learn to eat
whatever sustains you
until morning
but do not be misled by details
simply because you live them.

Do not let your head deny
your hands
any memory of what passes through them
nor your eyes
nor your heart
everything can be used
except what is wasteful
(you will need
to remember this when you are accused of destruction.)
Even when they are dangerous
examine the heart of those machines you hate
before you discard them
and never mourn the lack of their power
lest you be condemned
to relive them.

If you do not learn to hate
you will never be lonely
enough
to love easily
nor will you always be brave
although it does not grow any easier.
Do not pretend to convenient beliefs
even when they are righteous
you will never be able to defend your city
while shouting.

Remember our sun
is not the most noteworthy star
only the nearest.

Respect whatever pain you bring back
from your dreaming
but do not look for new gods
in the sea
nor in any part of a rainbow.
Each time you love
love as deeply
as if it were
forever
only nothing is
eternal.

Speak proudly to your children
where ever you may find them
tell them
you are the offspring of slaves
and your mother was
a princess
in darkness.

Uhuru

MARI EVANS

Fingers
flaming interclenched
blood to blood
The cold breath of our laughter
but a single wind
Your eye warm to mine shared
presentpast and ancient source
Black unison
our heartbeats

Dream Farmer

JILL WITHERSPOON BOYER

We are landless dream farmers
and when we only pluck at air
our surging spirit marks the land.
The fired hopes of centuries
guide our way persistently,
and ancient pains star concrete reality
with remembrances of joyous seasons.

We are dream farmers
the rainbow tribes
who mock the unyielding
and labor with the faith
of desert blooms.

When Brothers Forget
JILL WITHERSPOON BOYER

when brothers forget
         come bombs
         and politics.
come creeds
that send the armies marching.
sitting down to tea
inspires only plotting
and men clasp hands
     to give the sign
     before tomorrow's battle.
when brothers forget
warmth watches at the edge of the world
waiting for them
who have gone too far away—
like mama leaning out the window
calling her children home

Do Not Think
CAROL FREEMAN

Do not think
We
Want to harm you
if
We touch
Your
Confused mind

And
Pull you into
Blackness
—we only want to bring you home.

SOS

AMIRI BARAKA (LEROI JONES)

Calling black people
Calling all black people, man woman child
Wherever you are, calling you, urgent, come in
Black People, come in, wherever you are, urgent, calling
you, calling all black people
calling all black people, come in, black people, come
on in.

(on the naming day)

JOHARI M. KUNJUFU

you come
in ancestral wisdom of the round moon
waiting by elephant bush
where we will pass again
to touch the baobab
and feed old drums
when our parched flesh is renewed
and the sun moves as gold bands on the grasslands

Sudan child there is a star
streaming east to sign the time of cleansing

for you our blood lives between the reed
and the palm
and beats in the soil of many days

libations flow

as the guinea corn is finely ground
in the way of a thousand stones
we take our own

Black People: This Is Our Destiny
AMIRI BARAKA (LEROI JONES)

The road runs straight with no turning, the circle
runs complete as it is in the storm of peace, the all
embraced embracing in the circle complete turning road
straight like a burning straight with the circle complete
as in a peaceful storm, the elements, the niggers' voices
harmonized with creation on a peak in the holy black man's
eyes that we rise, whose race is only direction up, where
we go to meet the realization of makers knowing who we are
and the war in our hearts but the purity of the holy world
that we long for, knowing how to live, and what life is, and
who God is, and the many revolutions we must spin through in our
seven adventures in the endlessness of all existing feeling, all
existing forms of life, the gases, the plants, the ghost minerals
the spirits the souls the light in the stillness where the storm
the glow the nothing in God is complete except there is nothing
to be incomplete the pulse and change of rhythm, blown flight
to be anything at all . . . vibration holy nuance beating against
itself, a rhythm a playing re-understood now by one of the 1st race
the primitives the first men who evolve again to civilize the
world

change-up

HAKI R. MADHUBUTI (DON L. LEE)

change-up,
let's go for ourselves
both cheeks are broken now.
change-up,
move past the corner bar,
let yr/spirit lift u above that quick high.
change-up,
that tooth pick you're sucking on was
once a log.
change-up,
and yr/children will look at u differently
than   we looked at our parents.

Five Men
Against the Theme
"My Name Is Red Hot.
Yo Name Ain Doodley Squat."

Hoyt and Lerone, Dudley and Haki and Lu.

GWENDOLYN BROOKS

This is the time of the crit, the creeple, and the makeiteer.

Our warfare is through the trite traitors, through
the ice-committees, through
the mirages, through
the suburban petals, through
toss-up, and tin-foil.

Therefore we are thankful for steel.
We
are thanful
for steel.

blackmen: who make morning

ANGELA JACKSON

for blackmen.
who reach. who peel the filthy shell of sky.
              who make the morning.
who hold. who turn fire in their hands
              balance water and woman
                                    wine within their palms
our fathers. tossing their tender seeds
                              against the barrenlands
                          across the far once fallow fields
                      who speak.
whose throats are raw with accusation.

who make no treaties with murderers.

who speak no compromise   no politeness/s.

for
our sons.
who whisper. who fill the pockets of our sorrow
                              with pieces of wind. and
                          comfort coins of courage.
who walk. in strength. in passion are relentless
          and dangerous. whose lines are narrow and clean
        are weary. and private. stalwart. and stunned by poisons
      often close to unkind: who are human and full.

these men. our lovers.

biting into the root of our anguish
who hone their discontents desperations into weapons
with their words
and with the hands of all our fathers
turn
and pull us to a rising.

with these fist/s
who bind our fury into this freedom

for our brothers!
we shout down heaven for history to hear.

because we have promised tomorrow to ourselves.

Patience of a People

F. J. BRYANT, JR.

It is our hand, the
Deepness of our eye, legs
Taut as a springboard
     That they forget

It is ridiculed curls,
Grim nights without moons,
Love, a family, arbitrary consent,
     That they forget

It is death at early ages,
Shabby homes with walls of fear,
The lie of our carefree ways
     That they forget

It is wide-eyed sight,
A silence that is not theirs, a
Fall bonfire in summer that only
     Lets one eye sleep

The Real People
Loves One Another
ROB PENNY

the real people loves one another
the rest bees shaming, bees walkin
backwards under the sun.

when black people are
A. B. SPELLMAN

when black people are
with each other
we sometimes fear ourselves
whisper over our shoulders
about unmentionable acts
& sometimes we fight & lie.
these are somethings we sometimes do.

& when alone i sometimes walk
from wall to wall fighting visions
of white men fighting me
& black men fighting white men
& fighting me & i lose my
self between walls &
ricocheting shots & can't say
for certain who i have killed
or been killed by.

it is the fear of winter passing
& summer coming & the killing
i have called for coming

to my door saying
hit it a.b., you're in it too.

& the white army moves like thieves
in the night mass producing beautiful
black corpses & then stealing them away
while my frequent death watches me
from orangeburg on cronkite &
i'm oiling my gun & cooking my food
& saying "when the time comes"
to myself, over & over, hopefully.

but i remember driving from atlanta
to the city with stone & featherstone
& cleve & on the way feather talked
about ambushing a pair of klansmen
& cleve told how they hunted
chaney's body in the white night
of the haunted house in the mississippi
swamp while a runaway survivor
from orangeburg slept between wars
on the back seat.
times like this
are times when black people
are with each other & the strength flows
back & forth between us like
borrowed breath.

For My People

MARGARET WALKER

For my people everywhere singing their slave songs
        repeatedly: their dirges and their ditties and their blues
        and jubilees, praying their prayers nightly to an

unknown god, bending their knees humbly to an
unseen power;

For my people lending their strength to the years, to the
gone years and the now years and the maybe years,
washing ironing cooking scrubbing sewing mending
hoeing plowing digging planting pruning patching
dragging along never gaining never reaping never
knowing and never understanding;

For my playmates in the clay and dust and sand of Alabama
backyards playing baptizing and preaching and doctor
and jail and soldier and school and mama and cooking
and playhouse and concert and store and hair and Miss
Choomby and company;

For the cramped bewildered years we went to school to
learn to know the reasons why and the answers to and
the people who and the places where and the days
when, in memory of the bitter hours when we
discovered we were black and poor and small and
different and nobody cared and nobody wondered and
nobody understood;

For the boys and girls who grew in spite of these things to
be man and woman, to laugh and dance and sing and
play and drink their wine and religion and success, to
marry their playmates and bear children and then die
of consumption and anemia and lynching;

For my people thronging 47th Street in Chicago and Lenox
Avenue in New York and Rampart Street in New
Orleans, lost disinherited dispossessed and happy
people filling the cabarets and taverns and other
people's pockets needing bread and shoes and milk
and land and money and something — something all our
own;

For my people walking blindly spreading joy, losing time
being lazy, sleeping when hungry, shouting when

burdened, drinking when hopeless, tied and shackled
and tangled among ourselves by the unseen creatures
who tower over us omnisciently and laugh;

For my people blundering and groping and floundering in
the dark of churches and schools and clubs and
societies, associations and councils and committees
and conventions, distressed and disturbed and deceived
and devoured by money-hungry glory-craving leeches,
preyed on by facile force of state and fad and novelty,
by false prophet and holy believer;

For my people standing staring trying to fashion a better
way from confusion, from hypocrisy and
misunderstanding, trying to fashion a world that will
hold all the people, all the faces, all the adams and
eves and their countless generations;

Let a new earth rise. Let another world be born. Let a
bloody peace be written in the sky. Let a second
generation full of courage issue forth; let a people
loving freedom come to growth. Let a beauty full of
healing and a strength of final clenching be the pulsing
in our spirits and our blood. Let the martial songs be
written, let the dirges disappear. Let a race of men now
rise and take control.

Biographical Notes

SAMUEL ALLEN (PAUL VESEY) was born in Columbus, Ohio, and is presently professor of English at Boston University. He is a renowned poet, lawyer, and teacher. His books include *Elfenbein Zähne (Ivory Tusks)* (1956), *Ivory Tusks* (1968), and *Paul Vesey's Ledger* (1975).

RUSSELL ATKINS is a native of Cleveland, Ohio, where he lives and teaches. He is founder and co-editor of the magazine, *Free Lance,* and his books include *Heretofore* (1968), and *Here In The* (1976).

ALVIN AUBERT was born in Lutcher, Louisiana, and is currently professor of English at the State University of New York at Fredonia. He is publisher and editor of *Obsidian: Black Literature in Review.* His books include *Against the Blues* (1972) and *Feeling Through* (1976).

AMIRI BARAKA (LEROI JONES) was born in Newark, New Jersey, and he is still involved in the social and political life of that city. He is publisher of Jihad Publications, founder of the Black Arts Repertory Theatre and Spirit House; and one of the most influential Black American writers of our time. His books of poetry include *Preface to a Twenty-Volume Suicide Note* (1961), *The Dead Lecturer* (1964), *Black Magic Poetry 1961 – 1967* (1969) and *Spirit, Reach* (1972).

GEORGE BARLOW is a native of Berkeley, California, and is teaching in the English Department at the University of California in that city. His work has appeared in numerous periodicals and anthologies; and a collection of his poetry, *Gabriel*, was published in 1974.

GERALD W. BARRAX was born in Attalla, Alabama, and is a member of the Department of English of North Carolina State University at Raleigh. His poetry has appeared in many anthologies, and a collection of his work, *Another Kind of Rain*, was published in 1970.

LERONE BENNETT is a noted historian, journalist and teacher. He is senior editor of *Ebony* magazine and author of such significant non-fiction works as *Before the Mayflower* (1962), *Pioneers in Protest* (1969), and *The Challenge of Blackness* (1972). His poetry has appeared in numerous anthologies, including *New Negro Poets* (1964), and *The Poetry of Black America* (1973).

ISAAC J. BLACK was raised in the housing projects of the Brownsville section of Brooklyn. He is the winner of numerous awards, has been a commercial artist, and works in rehabilitation projects in the field of drug addiction. His poetry has appeared in *Black World, Obsidian,* and *The Journal of Black Poetry.*

HENRY BLAKELY, a native of Chicago, Illinois, a novelist as well as poet, is married to poet Gwendolyn Brooks. *Windy Place*, a collection of his poetry, was published in 1974.

JULIAN BOND is a native Georgian, and a distinguished journalist, political leader, and civil rights activist. His poetry has been published in such anthologies as *American Negro Poetry* (1963), edited by Arna Bontemps. Mr. Bond is presently a member of the state senate of the state of Georgia.

ARNA BONTEMPS was born in Alexandria, Louisiana, and had a unique and distinguished career as author, poet, anthologist librarian, and teacher. His poetry anthologies include *The*

Poetry of the Negro (1949, 1970), which he edited with Langston Hughes, and *American Negro Poetry* (1963). A collection of his poems, *Personals,* was published in 1963.

SHARON BOURKE lives in New York City. Her poetry has appeared in *Understanding the New Black Poetry,* an anthology edited by Stephen Henderson in 1972. Her poem, "Sopranosound, Memory of John," was written to accompany the work of Black photographer Omar Kharem.

JILL WITHERSPOON BOYER was born and educated in Detroit, Michigan. Her work has appeared in *Journal of Black Poetry, The Broadside Annual, 1973,* and other anthologies and periodicals. Her book, *Dream Farmer,* was published in 1975.

LINDA BROWN BRAGG is a native of Akron, Ohio, the recipient of the Woodrow Wilson Fellowship, and a teacher at the University of North Carolina in Greensboro. Her work has appeared in numerous anthologies, including Rosey Pool's *Beyond the Blues* (1962). Her book, *A Love Song for Black Men* was published in 1974.

JODI BRAXTON was born in Lakeland, Maryland, and is a graduate of Sarah Lawrence College. She taught as a Danforth Fellow in the Department of English at Yale University and has been named to the University of Michigan Society of Fellows for further graduate study. Her first book of poetry, *Sometimes I Think of Maryland,* was published by Sunbury Press of New York City in 1977.

GWENDOLYN BROOKS was born in Topeka, Kansas, and raised in Chicago, Illinois, where she lives. In 1950 she received the Pulitzer Prize for poetry. Numerous other awards and honors have been presented to her during her distinguished career in literature. She has taught and lectured throughout the country. Her books of poetry include *A Street in Bronzeville* (1945), *Annie Allen* (1949), *The Bean Eaters* (1960), *Selected Poems*

(1966), *In the Mecca* (1968), *Riot* (1969), *Family Pictures* (1970), and *Beckoning* (1975).

STERLING A. BROWN was born and raised in Washington, D.C., and has had a long and distinguished teaching career at Howard University. He was senior editor of the landmark anthology of Black American literature, *The Negro Caravan* (1941, 1969), and has authored other books of literary criticism. His poetry was collected in *Southern Road,* published in 1932 and reissued in 1974. His poem "An Old Woman Remembers" refers to the Atlanta riot of 1906.

F. J. BRYANT, JR. was born in Philadelphia, Pennsylvania, and attended Lincoln University. His work has appeared in such periodicals as *Black World* and *Journal of Black Poetry* and in numerous anthologies, including *Black Fire* (1968) and *The Poetry of Black America* (1973). A volume of his poetry, *Songs from Ragged Streets,* was published in 1974.

JOHN HENRIK CLARKE was born in Union Springs, Alabama, and is a renowned author, anthologist, historian, and teacher. He is a professor at Hunter College in New York City, and editor of *Freedomways* magazine. He is the editor of *Harlem U.S.A.* (1971), *American Negro Short Stories* (1966), *Malcolm X: The Man and His Time* (1969) and numerous other collections. His poetry has been published in a volume entitled *Rebellion in Rhyme* (1948).

CAROLE GREGORY CLEMMONS is a native of Youngstown, Ohio, and graduated from Youngstown State University. Her poetry has been published in many periodicals and such anthologies as *Nine Black Poets* (1968), *The New Black Poetry* (1969), *A Galaxy of Black Writing* (1970), and *The Poetry of Black America* (1973).

LUCILLE CLIFTON was born in Depew, New York, and has published many books for children and young people. Her poetry has appeared in many periodicals and anthologies and in her collections, *Good Times* (1969) and *Good News About the Earth* (1972).

LLOYD CORBIN (DJANGATOLUM) was born in New York City and is a graduate of Brandeis University. His work has been published in numerous periodicals and in the anthologies, *The Me Nobody Knows* (1969), *Soulscript* (1970), *Black Out Loud* (1970), and *The Poetry of Black America* (1973).

SAM CORNISH was born in Baltimore, Maryland, and has been a teacher in that city and, more recently, in Boston, Massachusetts. He is the author of several books for children, including *Your Hand in Mine* (1969). His poetry has appeared in such publications as *Journal of Black Poetry* and *Massachusetts Review*. A collection of his poetry, *Generations*, was published in 1970.

STANLEY CROUCH was born in Los Angeles, California, and is a teacher and musician, as well as a poet. His work has appeared in such publications as *Black World* and *Liberator* and in the anthologies *Black Fire* (1968) and *The Poetry of Black America* (1973). A collection of his poetry, *Ain't No Ambulances for No Nigguhs Tonight*, was published in 1972.

MARGARET DANNER was born in Pryorsburg, Kentucky, and has won many awards; she has also taught and lectured throughout the country. She was a founder of Boone House for the Arts, in Detroit, and has been active in the presentation of Black arts of all kinds. Her published works include *Impressions of African Art Forms in Poetry* (1962); *To Flower* (1962); *Poem Counterpoem* (1966), a joint effort with Dudley Randall; and *Iron Lace* (1968).

OWEN DODSON was born in New York City and for many years was professor of Drama at Howard University. His plays have been produced in Europe and America, and his poetry and stories have been included in numerous anthologies. His books of poetry include *Powerful Long Ladder* (1946) and *The Confession Stone: Song Cycles* (1970).

HENRY DUMAS was born in Arkansas and raised in New York City where he was living in 1968 when he was shot and killed by a policeman. He was a teacher at Hiram College in Ohio, and his work had appeared in numerous periodicals and in such anthologies as *A Galaxy of Black Writing* (1970), *Black Out Loud* (1970), and *The Poetry of Black America* (1973). *Ark of Bones and Other Stories* and a collection of his poetry, *Play Ebony Play Ivory*, were published in 1974.

JAMES A. EMANUEL was born in Nebraska and is a professor of English at the City College of New York. His work has appeared in such periodicals as *The New York Times* and *Black World;* and in a variety of anthologies, including *New Negro Poets:USA* (1964) and *The Poetry of Black America* (1973). His collections of poetry include *The Treehouse and Other Poems* (1968) and *Panther Man* (1970).

MARI EVANS was born in Toledo, Ohio, and resides in Indianapolis, Indiana, where she writes and teaches. Her work has won many awards and appeared in numerous periodicals and anthologies. She is the author of notable books for children and young people, including *J.D.* (1973, 1975), *I Look At Me* (1974), and *Singing Black* (1976). Her books of poetry include *Where Is All the Music* (1968) and *I Am a Black Woman* (1970).

SARAH WEBSTER FABIO was born in Nashville, Tennessee, and is a member of the Afro-American Studies Department at the University of Wisconsin. Her work has appeared in a variety of periodicals and anthologies; and her collections of poetry include, *A Mirror: A Soul* (1969), *Black Is a Panther Caged* (1972), and *Jujus: Alchemy of the Blues* (1976).

JULIA FIELDS was born in Uniontown, Alabama, and was graduated from Knoxville College in Tennessee. Her work has appeared in such periodicals as *Black World, Umbra,* and the *Massachusetts Review:* and in a number of anthologies, including *Beyond the Blues* (1962), *City in All Directions* (1969), *The Poetry of the Negro* (1970), and *The Poetry of Black America* (1973).

CAROL FREEMAN was born in Rayville, Louisana, and makes her home in California, where she writes and lives. Her poetry has appeared in such anthologies as *Black Fire* (1968), *The Poetry of the Negro* (1970), and *The Poetry of Black America* (1973).

ZACK GILBERT was born near McMullin, Missouri, and spent most of his adult years in Chicago. His work has been published in such periodicals as *Black World* and *Liberator;* and in such anthologies as *For Malcolm* (1967), *The Poetry of the Negro* (1949, 1970), and *The Poetry of Black America* (1973).

NIKKI GIOVANNI was born in Knoxville, Tennessee, and raised in Cincinnati, Ohio. Her work has appeared in numerous periodicals and anthologies, and she has lectured widely around the country. Books of her poetry include *Black Feeling, Black Talk* (1968), *Black Judgement* (1968), *Re:Creation* (1970), *Spin a Soft Black Song* (1971), *My House* (1972), and *The Men and The Women* (1975).

MICHAEL S. HARPER was born in Brooklyn, New York, and grew up in Los Angeles. He has taught at colleges in California and is presently on the faculty of Brown University in Providence, Rhode Island. His work has appeared in numerous anthologies, and his collections of poetry include *Dear John, Dear Coltrane* (1970), *History Is Your Own Heartbeat* (1971), *History as Apple Tree* (1972), *Song: I Want a Witness* (1972), *Debridement* (1973), *Nightmare Begins Responsibility* (1975), and *Images of Kin* (1977).

WILLIAM J. HARRIS was born and raised in Yellow Springs, Ohio, and has taught creative writing and American literature at Cornell University. He has published poetry in *The American Scholar, Chicago Review,* and other periodicals; and his work has been in various anthologies, including *The Poetry of Black America* (1973). His published books of poetry are *Hey Fella, Would You Mind Holding This Piano a Moment* (1975) and *In My Own Dark Way* (1977).

ROBERT HAYDEN was born in Detroit, Michigan, is on the faculty of the University of Michigan at Ann Arbor, and is the Consultant in Poetry to the Library of Congress. He has received many honors and awards throughout a distinguished career. His collections of poetry include *A Ballad of Remembrance* (1962), *Selected Poems* (1966), *Words in the Mourning Time* (1972), and *Angle of Ascent: New and Selected Poems* (1975).

DAVID HENDERSON was born in Harlem, New York, has taught and lectured at a number of colleges around the country, and is presently writing and teaching in Berkeley, California. His poetry has appeared in such periodicals as *Evergreen Review, New American Review, Black World, Freedomways,* and *Journal of Black Poetry;* and in numerous anthologies. His books of poetry include *Felix of the Silent Forest* (1967), and *De Mayor of Harlem* (1971).

CALVIN C. HERNTON was born in Chattanooga, Tennessee, and is presently associate professor of Black Studies at Oberlin College in Ohio. His work has been included in many anthologies, and he is the author of several influential books of prose, including *Sex and Racism in America* (1964), *White Papers for White Americans* (1966), and *Coming Together: Black Power, White Hate and Sexual Hang ups* (1971). His books of poetry include *The Coming of Chronos to the House of Nightsong* (1963) and *Medicine Man* (1976). A novel, *Scarecrow,* was published in 1974.

EVERETT HOAGLAND was educated at Lincoln University in Pennsylvania, and at Brown University in Providence, Rhode Island. His work has appeared in such periodicals as *The American Poetry Review, First World, The Massachusetts Review,* and *Black World.* His collection of love poetry, *Black Velvet,* was published in 1970. He is presently a professor of English at Southeastern Massachusetts University at North Dartmouth, Massachusetts.

LANGSTON HUGHES was born in Joplin, Missouri, and was a prolific writer of poetry, stories and plays for over forty years. His international reputation as an influential Black American poet was established by such books as *The Weary Blues* (1926), *The Dream Keeper* (1932), *Montage of a Dream Deferred* (1951), *Selected Poems* (1969), *Ask Your Mama* (1961), and *The Panther and the Lash* (1967). His landmark poetry anthologies include *The Poetry of the Negro* (1949, 1970), which he edited with Arna Bontemps, and *New Negro Poets, USA* (1964). Langston Hughes died in 1967.

ANGELA JACKSON is an active member of the OBAC Writers Workshop in Chicago. Her poetry has appeared in numerous periodicals, including *Black World, First World, NOMMO,* and the *Chicago Review.* A book of her poetry, *VooDoo/Love Magic,* was published in 1974.

MAE JACKSON was born in Earl, Arkansas, and presently lives in New York City with her daughter, Njeri Ayoka. Her work has appeared in such periodicals as *Black World, Journal of Black Poetry,* and *Essence* and in the anthologies, *Night Comes Softly* (1970), *Black Out Loud* (1970), *Black Spirits* (1972), and *The Poetry of Black America* (1973). A collection of her poetry, *Can I Poet with You,* was published in 1969.

LANCE JEFFERS was born in Fremont, Nebraska, and has been an influential poet and teacher for over two decades. His poetry has appeared in numerous periodicals and anthologies of

Black American writing, and his collections of poetry include *My Blackness is the Beauty of This Land* (1970) and *When I Know the Power of My Black Hand* (1974).

TED JOANS was born in Cairo, Illinois, and is a painter and jazz musician, who has lived for many years in Europe and Africa. His work has appeared in many journals and anthologies, and his books of poetry include *Black Pow-Wow* (1969) and *Afrodisia* (1970).

FRED JOHNSON was born in Philadelphia, Pennsylvania, and is professor of English at Rutgers University. His work has appeared in such periodicals as *Cimarron Review* and *The Christian Science Monitor;* and in the anthologies, *Poems by Blacks III* and *The Poetry of Black America* (1973).

JOE JOHNSON was born in New York City, where he presently lives with his wife and young son. He teaches at Ramapo College in New York, and is involved in the publishing company of Reed, Cannon, and Johnson. His work has appeared in such periodicals as *Black Box, Hoodoo, Open Poetry, The Yardbird Reader;* and in the anthology, *The Poetry of Black America* (1973).

BOB KAUFMAN was born in San Francisco and was a leading poet during that city's literary "renaissance" of the 1950s. He was also influential in the development of "beat" poetry of that period. His work was greatly respected in England and on the Continent before becoming well known in America. He is represented in a variety of anthologies, and his collections of poetry include *Solitudes Crowded with Loneliness* (1965) and *Golden Sardine* (1967).

ETHERIDGE KNIGHT was born in Corinth, Mississippi, and had his first collection of poems, *Poems from Prison* (1968), published while he was still an inmate at Indiana State Prison. His work has appeared in numerous anthologies and periodicals, including *Black World, Journal of Black Poetry, City in All Directions* (1969), *The New Black Poetry* (1969), *Dices or Black Bones* (1970), and *The Poetry of Black America* (1973). A collection of his poetry, *Belly Song,* was published in 1973.

JOHARI M. KUNJUFU (formerly JOHARI M. AMINI) was born in Philadelphia, Pennsylvania, and educated in Chicago, Illinois. She is an essayist, the editor of *Black Books Bulletin,* and a lecturer in Black Literature. Her publications include *Images in Black* (1967), *Black Essence* (1968), *A Folk Fable* (1969), *Lets Go Some Where* (1970), and *A Hip Tale in the Death Style* (1972).

REGINALD LOCKETT was born in Berkeley, California. He is presently a lecturer in creative writing at San Francisco State University and is the editor of *Folio,* a magazine published by radio station KPFA in Berkeley. His poetry has appeared in such periodicals as *Black World, Iowa Review, Soulbook, Black Dialogue,* and in numerous anthologies. A book of his poetry, *Oakland Flash,* was published in 1977.

ELOUISE LOFTIN was born in Brooklyn, New York, and was educated at New York University, where she was poetry editor of *Black Creation* magazine. Her work has been published in the periodicals *Essence, Présence Africaine,* and *Confrontation,* and in such anthologies as *The Poetry of Black America* (1973). Her first collection of poetry, *Jumbish,* was published in 1972.

PEARL CLEAGE LOMAX was born in Springfield, Massachusetts, and was educated at Howard University and at Spelman College, where she had her plays produced. Her poetry has appeared in numerous periodicals and anthologies. A collection of her poetry, *We Don't Need No Music,* was published in 1972.

DOUGHTRY LONG was born in Atlanta, Georgia, and has traveled and lived in Africa. His work has appeared in such periodicals as *Black World, Essence, Chelsea Magazine;* and in the anthologies *The Black Poets* (1971) and *The Poetry of Black America* (1973). Collections of his poetry include *Black Love, Black Hope* (1970) and *Song for Nia* (1971).

AUDRE LORDE was born in New York City and presently writes and teaches in that area. Her work has appeared in numerous periodicals and anthologies. Her books of poetry include *The First Cities* (1968), *Cables To Rage* (1970), *From a Land Where Other People Live* (1973), *New York Head Shop and Museum* (1974), and *Coal* (1976).

K. CURTIS LYLE was born in Los Angeles and makes his home in northern California, where he works with young authors in the "Poets in the Schools" program. He was an original member of the Watts Writers' Workshop and his work has appeared in numerous periodicals and anthologies, including *Black World, The Poetry of Black America* (1973) and *Giant Talk* (1975). His books of poetry include *Drunk on God* and *From Out of Nowhere* (1974) and *Fifteen Predestination Weather Reports* (1977).

CHARLES LYNCH was born in Baltimore, Maryland, and makes his home in New York City, where he is professor of English at the Center for Labor Studies. He is an editor of *Forms,* a magazine of poetry and graphics, and his work has appeared in numerous periodicals, including *Yardbird Reader, Journal of Black Poetry, Sunbury, Perspective, Obsidian,* and *The Greenfield Review.*

NATE MACKEY was born in Miami, Florida, and is presently a member of the Department of English at the University of Southern California at Los Angeles. His work has appeared in various periodicals, including *Black World, Gumbo, Yardbird Reader,* and *Brilliant Corners.* He is editor of *Hambone* magazine and is completing work on a first collection of poetry, *The Various Burning.*

HAKI R. MADHUBUTI (DON L. LEE) was born in Little Rock, Arkansas, and is a critic, teacher, and essayist, as well as a poet. His work has been included in a number of anthologies and periodicals, and his books of poetry include *Think Black!* (1967), *Black Pride* (1968), *Don't Cry, Scream* (1969), *We Walk the Way of the New World* (1970), and *Directionscore: Selected and New Poems* (1971). He is an editor at Third World Press and the founder of the Institute of Positive Education, both in Chicago.

BARBARA MAHONE was born in Chicago and currently resides in Atlanta, Georgia, with her daughter, Letta Kilolo. Her work has appeared in such periodicals as *Black World, Nommo,* and *Tuesday;* and in the anthologies *Night Comes Softly* (1970) and *The Poetry of Black America* (1973). Her collection of poetry, *Sugarfields,* was published in 1970.

GLORIA ODEN was born in Yonkers, New York, and educated at Howard University, where she received a degree in law. She has been a book and magazine editor and taught at the State University of New York at Stony Brook. She is presently professor of English at the University of Maryland, Baltimore County. Her work has appeared in a variety of periodicals and anthologies and in a joint volume with May Swenson, *Poetry Is Alive and Well and Living in America.*

OLUMO (JIM CUNNINGHAM) was born in Webster Groves, Missouri, but grew up in St. Louis. He currently lives in Daytona Beach, Florida, where he writes and teaches. His work has appeared in such periodicals as *Black World;* and in the anthologies *Jump Bad* (1971), *To Gwen with Love* (1971) and *New Black Voices* (1972), among others. He has published a first collection of his poetry, *The Blue Narrator.*

Bob O'Meally was born in Washington, D.C., and is presently a professor of English and director of the Honors Program at Howard University. His work has appeared in such Journals as *The Harvard Advocate, Obsidian,* and *Janus;* and in the anthology, *My Black Me* (1974).

Lindsay Patterson was born in Bastrop, Louisiana, and writes fiction and critical essays on American literature and film, as well as being a poet and anthologist. His poetry has appeared in a variety of periodicals and anthologies, and he has received several fellowships and awards. In 1973 he published *A Rock Against the Wind,* an anthology of Black love poems.

Raymond R. Patterson was born in New York City and resides there as a teacher, editor and poet. His poetry has appeared in such anthologies as *Beyond the Blues* (1962), *For Malcolm* (1967), *I Am the Darker Brother* (1968), *Black Out Loud* (1970), *The Poetry of the Negro* (1949, 1970), and *The Poetry of Black America* (1973). A collection of his poetry, *26 Ways of Looking at a Black Man,* was published in 1969. He is presently a lecturer in English at the City College of New York.

Rob Penny was born in Opelika, Alabama, and is presently a professor in the Department of Black Community Education, Research, and Development at the University of Pittsburgh. He is Playwright-in-Residence at the Kuntu Repertory Theatre of Pittsburgh, where four of his plays have been produced. A collection of his poetry, *Black Tones of Truth,* was published in 1970.

Frank Lamont Phillips was born in Eloy, Arizona, raised in St. Louis, Missouri, and Alton, Illinois, and is presently a member of the United States Coast Guard. His poetry has appeared in such publications as *New Letters, Essence, Black World, The Broadside Annual, 1973,* and the revised edition of *American Negro Poetry* (1974).

STERLING D. PLUMPP was born in Clinton, Mississippi, and is presently an instructor in the Black Studies Program of the University of Illinois at the Chicago Circle Campus. His work has appeared in numerous periodicals and anthologies, and his collections of poetry include *Portable Soul* (1969), *Half Black, Half Blacker* (1970), *Muslim Men* (1972), *Black Rituals* (1972) and *Steps to Break the Circle* (1974).

DUDLEY RANDALL was born in Washington, D.C., and he has been a librarian, anthologist, poet, and publisher of Black American poetry for many years. He is the founder of Broadside Press, a pioneering Black publishing company which has presented many important contributions to Black American literature during the 1960s and 1970s. His work has been widely anthologized. His poetry collections include *Poem, Counterpoem* (1966) with Margaret Danner; *Cities Burning* (1968); *Love You* (1971); *More to Remember* (1971); and *After the Killing* (1973).

EUGENE REDMOND was born in East St. Louis, Illinois, and is presently an English professor and Poet-in-Residence at the University of California at Sacramento. His poetry has appeared in a wide variety of periodicals. Some of his collections of poetry include *Sentry of the Four Golden Pillars* (1970), *River of Bones and Flesh and Blood* (1971), and *Consider Loneliness as These Things* (1974). He is the author of a unique critical history of Black American poetry entitled *Drumvoices: The Mission of Afro-American Poetry*, published in 1977.

ISHMAEL REED was born in Chattanooga, Tennessee, and makes his home in Berkeley, California. He is a novelist, essayist, and teacher, as well as a poet, and his work has appeared in a variety of periodicals and anthologies. He is the editor of an anthology, *19 Necromancers from Now* (1970); the publisher of books by Reed, Cannon, and Johnson; and the editor of the *Yardbird Reader* series, begun in 1972. His volumes of poetry include *catechism of d neoamerican hoodoo church* (1971), *Selected Poems* (1972), and *Conjure* (1972).

CONRAD KENT RIVERS was born in Atlantic City, New Jersey, and was a resident of Chicago and a teacher in the Gary, Indiana, school system at the time of his sudden death in 1968. His work has appeared in numerous periodicals and anthologies, including *American Negro Poetry* (1963) and *The Poetry of Black America* (1973). His volumes of poetry include *Perchance to Dream Othello* (1959), *These Black Bodies and This Sunburnt Face* (1962), *Dusk at Selma* (1965), and *The Still Voice of Harlem* (1968).

CAROLYN M. RODGERS was born and raised in Chicago, Illinois, and has been involved in the literary life of that city. Her work has appeared in many periodicals and anthologies, and some of her books of poetry include *Paper Soul* (1968), *Songs of a Blackbird* (1969), *Blues Gittin Up* (1972), and *How I Got Ovah* (1975).

CHARLES ROWELL was born in Auburn, Alabama, and is a member of the Department of English at Southern University in Baton Rouge, Louisiana. He is an editor of *Callaloo*, a new journal of southern Black writing, and his work has appeared in such publications as *Black World*, *Obsidian*, and *Southern Humanities Review*.

SONIA SANCHEZ was born in Birmingham, Alabama. Her work has been widely anthologized. She has also written plays and stories and edited anthologies of Black American literature. She has lectured widely around the country and taught at several universities. Her collections of poetry include *Homecoming* (1969), *We a Baddddd People* (1970), *It's a New Day: Poems for Young Brothas and Sistuhs* (1971), *Three Hundred and Sixty Degrees of Blackness Comin at You* (1972), and *A Blues Book for Blue Black Magical Women* (1974).

JUDY DOTHARD SIMMONS was born in Westerly, Rhode Island, and makes her home in Mount Vernon, New York. She teaches and lectures at colleges around the country and has been involved in drama and the business world. Her poetry has appeared in a variety of periodicals including *Encore, Poet Lore, Black Box, 1972;* and in such anthologies as *Understanding the New Black Poetry* (1973) and *Giant Talk* (1975). Her collection of poetry, *Judith's Blues,* was published in 1973.

A. B. SPELLMAN is a jazz critic and historian, as well as a poet. His work has appeared in such periodicals as *Journal of Black Poetry, The Nation, Metronome,* and *Umbra.* He is represented in a variety of anthologies, including *Beyond the Blues* (1972), *New Negro Poets: USA* (1964), *Black Fire* (1968), *The New Black Poetry* (1969), *Dices or Black Bones* (1970), and *The Poetry of Black America* (1973). He is the author of a book of essays on jazz musicians, *Four Lives in the Bebop Business (1966),* and of a volume of poetry, *The Beautiful Days* (1965).

JOYCE CAROL THOMAS lives in Berkeley, California, where she writes and teaches Spanish. Her poetry has appeared in such periodicals as *The Yardbird Reader* and in the anthology, *Giant Talk* (1965). A collection of her poetry, *Bittersweet,* was published in 1973.

QUINCY TROUPE was born in New York City and raised in St. Louis. He presently lives in New York City and teaches at the College of Staten Island and at the Frederick Douglass Creative Arts Center in Harlem. His poetry has appeared in a wide variety of periodicals, including *Essence, Encore, Black World, Sumac, New Directions 22, Sunbury, The Yardbird Reader,* and *Mundus Artium.* He was the founding editor of *Confrontation: A Journal of Third World Literature* while on the faculty of Ohio University. He is a contributing editor of such publications as *Bopp, Mundus Artium, Okike,* and *The Yardbird Reader.* He is co-editor of *Giant Talk: An Anthology* of *Third World Writings* (1975); and his collections of poetry include *Embryo* (1972), *Ash Doors and Juju Guitars* (forthcoming), and *Edges* (forthcoming).

MARGARET WALKER was born in Birmingham, Alabama, and has been a member of the faculty of Jackson State College in Jackson, Mississippi, for many years. Her work has appeared in numerous periodicals and anthologies, and she has lectured widely around the country. Her novel, *Jubilee* (1977) was a recipient of the Houghton-Mifflin Literary Fellowship. Her collections of poetry include *For My People* (1942), a Yale University Younger Poets volume for that year, and *Prophets for a New Day* (1970).

RON WELBURN was born in Bryn Mawr, Pennsylvania, and graduated from Lincoln University in that state. His poetry and fiction have appeared in numerous periodicals and anthologies. He has taught at Syracuse University and at the Auburn Correctional Facility in New York. His books of poetry include *Peripheries* (1972) and *Brownup* (forthcoming).

AL YOUNG was born in Ocean Springs, Mississippi, grew up in Detroit, Michigan, and makes his home in Palo Alto, California, where he writes and teaches. His novels include *Snakes* (1970), *Who is Angelina* (1975), and *Sitting Pretty* (1976, 1977). His collections of poetry include *Dancing* (1969), *The Song Turning Back into Itself 3* (1971), and *Geography of the Near Past* (1976).

YVONNE lives in Riverdale, New York, and is presently an editor at *Ms.* magazine. She is a former editor of *Aphra* magazine, and her poetry has been published in such periodicals as *New York Quarterly*, *Ms.*, *Aphra*, *Obsidian*, and *Sunbury*. Her work is included in the anthologies *Anthology of New American Verse* (1974), *We Become New* (1975), *New American Poets* (1977), *Woman Song* (1977), and *Sisters of the Word: Anthology of New Women Poets* (forthcoming).

Acknowledgments (continued from page iv)

GERALD W. BARRAX: "If She Sang" from Black World, September 1973. Copyright © 1973 by Gerald W. Barrax. Reprinted by permission of Black World, Johnson Publishing Company, and Gerald W. Barrax. "Your Eyes Have Their Silence," and "For Malcolm: After Mecca" from Another Kind of Rain by Gerald W. Barrax (University of Pittsburgh Press). Copyright © 1970 by Gerald W. Barrax. Reprinted with permission of the University of Pittsburgh Press.

LERONE BENNETT: "And Was Not Improved" reprinted by permission of Lerone Bennett.

ISAAC J. BLACK: "Roll Call: A Land of Old Folks and Children," "Talking to the Townsfolk in Ideal, Georgia" from Black World, December 1975. Copyright © 1975. Reprinted by permission of Black World, Johnson Publishing Company, and Isaac J. Black.

HENRY BLAKELY: "Morning Song," and "H. Rapp Brown" from Windy Place by Henry Blakely (Broadside Press). Copyright © 1974. Reprinted by permission of Broadside Press.

JULIAN BOND: "The Bishop of Atlanta: Ray Charles" from American Negro Poetry edited by Arna Bontemps (Hill & Wang). Copyright © 1963. Reprinted by permission of Julian Bond.

ARNA BONTEMPS: "Southern Mansion" from Personals by Arna Bontemps (Paul Bremen, London). Copyright © 1963 by Arna Bontemps. Reprinted by permission of Harold Ober Associates, Inc.

SHARON BOURKE: "Sopranosound, Memory of John" from Understanding the New Black Poetry by Stephen Henderson (Morrow). Copyright © 1972 by Stephen Henderson. Reprinted with permission of Stephen Henderson and Sharon J. Bourke.

JILL WITHERSPOON BOYER: "Detroit City," "King Lives," "Dream Farmer," and "When Brothers Forget" from Dream Farmer by Jill Witherspoon Boyer (Broadside Press). Copyright © 1975 by Jill Witherspoon Boyer. Reprinted by permission of Broadside Press.

LINDA BROWN BRAGG: "A Poem About Beauty, Blackness, Poetry," and "Our Blackness Did Not Come to Us Whole" from A Love Song to Black Men by Linda Brown Bragg (Broadside Press). Copyright © 1974. Reprinted by permission of Broadside Press.

JODI BRAXTON: "sometimes i think of maryland" from Black World, November 1974. Copyright © 1977 by Joanne M. Braxton. Reprinted by permission of Black World, Johnson Publishing Company, and Joanne M. Braxton.

GWENDOLYN BROOKS: "Boys. Black./A Preachment," "Friend," "Horses Graze," "A Black Wedding Song," and "Five Men Against the Theme/'My Name is Red Hot./Yo Name Ain Doodley Squat' " from Beckonings by Gwendolyn Brooks (Broadside Press). Copyright © 1975. Reprinted by permission of Broadside Press. "The Last Quatrain of the Ballad of Emmett Till," and "Malcolm X" from The World of Gwendolyn Brooks by Gwendolyn Brooks (Harper & Row). "The Last Quatrain of the Ballad of Emmett Till" copyright © 1960 by Gwendolyn Brooks. "Malcolm X" copyright © 1967 by Gwendolyn Brooks. Both poems reprinted with permission of Harper & Row, Publishers, Inc. "Paul Robeson," and "Martin Luther King, Jr." from Family Pictures (Broadside Press). Reprinted by permission of Broadside Press.

STERLING A. BROWN: "Strong Men" and "Strange Legacies" from *Southern Road* by Sterling A. Brown (Harcourt, 1932; Beacon Press, 1974). Copyright © 1974 by Sterling A. Brown and reprinted with his permission. "An Old Woman Remembers" copyright © by Sterling A. Brown and reprinted with his permission.

F. J. BRYANT, JR.: "Patience of a People" copyright © by F. J. Bryant, Jr. and reprinted with his permission.

JOHN HENRIK CLARKE: "Determination" from *Rebellion in Rhyme* by John Henrik Clarke. Copyright © 1948 by John Henrik Clarke and reprinted with his permission.

CAROLE GREGORY CLEMMONS: "Love from My Father" from *Nine Black Poets,* edited by R. Baird Shuman (Moore). Copyright © 1968 by Moore Publishing Company, Durham, North Carolina, and reprinted with their permission.

LUCILLE CLIFTON: "Untitled" from *Black World,* December 1973. Copyright © 1974 by Lucille Clifton. Reprinted by permission of *Black World,* Johnson Publishing Company, and Lucille Clifton. "Africa," "listen children," "The Raising of Lazarus," "to Bobby Seale," "God Send Easter," and "Malcolm" from *Good News About the Earth,* by Lucille Clifton (Random House). Copyright © 1970, 1971, 1972 by Lucille Clifton. Reprinted by permission of Random House, Inc., and Curtis Brown, Ltd. "Miss Rosie," "For deLawd," "Good Times," "in the inner city," and "Those Boys That Ran Together" from *Good Times,* by Lucille Clifton (Random House). Copyright © 1969 by Lucille Clifton. Reprinted by permission of Random House, Inc.

LLOYD CORBIN (DJANGATOLUM): "Ali" reprinted by permission of Lloyd M. Corbin, Jr.

ELOUISE LOFTIN: "Pigeon" first appeared in *Black World* and is reprinted with permission of *Black World,* Johnson Publishing Company, and Elouise Loftin.

SAM CORNISH: "Your Mother," "Home," "April 68," "Lenox Christmas Eve 68," "Sooner or Later," "A Black Man," "Ray Charles," "Dory Miller," "Montgomery," and "Death of Dr. King" from *Generations,* by Sam Cornish (Beacon Press). Copyright © 1968, 1969, 1970, 1971 by Sam Cornish. Reprinted by permission of Beacon Press. "Sam's World" from *Natural Process: An Anthology of New Black Poetry,* edited by Ted Wilentz and Tom Weatherly (Hill & Wang). Copyright © 1970 by Hill & Wang, Inc. Reprinted with permission of Hill & Wang (now a division of Farrar, Straus & Giroux, Inc.).

STANLEY CROUCH: "After the Rain" from *Ain't No Ambulances for No Nigguhs Tonight,* by Stanley Crouch (Richard Baron Publishing Co.). Reprinted with permission of Richard W. Baron.

MARGARET DANNER: "A Grandson is a Hoticeberg" from *Black World.* Reprinted by permission of *Black World,* Johnson Publishing Company, and Margaret Danner.

OWEN DODSON: "For Edwin R. Embree," and "Yardbird's Skull" reprinted by permission of Owen Dodson.

HENRY DUMAS: "Black Star Line," and "knock on wood" from *Play Ebony Play Ivory,* by Henry Dumas (Random House). Copyright © 1974 by Loretta Dumas. Reprinted by permission of Random House, Inc.

JAMES A. EMANUEL: "Emmett Till" copyright © 1963 by The New York Times Company. Reprinted by their permission. "Negritude," and "Emmett Till" from *The Treehouse,* by James A. Emanuel (Broadside Press). Copyright © 1968, and reprinted with the permission of Broadside Press.

MARI EVANS: "Who Can Be Born Black," "I Am A Black Woman," and "Uhuru" from *I Am a Black Woman*, by Mari Evans (William Morrow). Copyright © 1970 by Mari Evans. Reprinted by permission of Mari Evans. "Langston" from *Free Lance*. Copyright by Mari Evans, and reprinted with her permission.

SARAH WEBSTER FABIO: "Chromo" from *Jujus/Alchemy of the Blues*, by Sarah Webster Fabio (A Rainbow Sign Volumn). Copyright © 1976 by Sarah Webster Fabio. Reprinted by permission of Sarah Webster Fabio.

JULIA FIELDS: "Harlem in January," "High on the Hog," and "A Poem for Heroes" reprinted by permission of Julia Fields, "Aardvark" from *Nine Black Poets*, edited by R. Baird Shuman (Moore). Copyright © 1968 by Moore Publishing Company, Durham, N.C., and reprinted with their permission.

CAROL FREEMAN: "Do Not Think" from *Black Fire*, edited by LeRoi Jones and Larry Neal (Morrow). Copyright © 1968. Reprinted by permission of The Sterling Lord Agency, Inc.

ZACK GILBERT: "O.D." from *My Own Hallelujahs*, by Zack Gilbert (Third World Press). Copyright © 1971 by Third World Press and reprinted with their permission.

NIKKI GIOVANNI: "Knoxville, Tennessee," and "Dreams" from *Black Feeling Black Talk Black Judgement*, by Nikki Giovanni (Morrow). Copyright © 1968, 1970 by Nikki Giovanni. Reprinted by permission of William Morrow & Company, Inc. "Mothers," "A Certain Peace," "Scrapbooks," and "Untitled" from *My House*, by Nikki Giovanni (Morrow). Copyright © 1972 by Nikki Giovanni. Reprinted by permission of William Morrow & Company, Inc. "Revolutionary Dreams" from *Re:Creation*, by Nikki Giovanni (Broadside Press). Copyright © 1970 by Broadside Press and reprinted with their permission.

MICHAEL S. HARPER: "Cannon Arrested" from *Black World*, January 1976. Copyright © 1977 by Michael S. Harper and reprinted with his permission. "Effendi" from *Dear John, Dear Coltrane*, by Michael S. Harper (University of Pittsburgh Press). Copyright © 1970 by the University of Pittsburgh Press and reprinted with their permission. "The Dark Way Home: Survivors," "Martin's Blues," and "Here Where Coltrane Is" from *History Is Your Own Heartbeat*, by Michael S. Harper (University of Illinois Press). Copyright © 1971 by Michael S. Harper. Reprinted by permission of Michael S. Harper and the University of Illinois Press.

WILLIAM J. HARRIS: "Give Me Five" from *Chicago Review*, Vol. 26, No. 4, 1975. Copyright © 1975 by *Chicago Review*. Reprinted by permission of *Chicago Review* and the author. "A Grandfather Poem," and "Rib Sandwich" copyright © 1977 by William J. Harris and reprinted with his permission. "They Live in Parallel Worlds" copyright © 1975 by William J. Harris and reprinted with his permission.

ROBERT HAYDEN: "Beginnings (I, II, and III)," "Stars (III)," "Homage to the Empress of the Blues," "Runagate Runagate," "Crispus Attucks," "El-Hajj Malik El-Shabazz (Malcolm X)," "Frederick Douglass," "Those Winter Sundays," from *Angle of Ascent, New and Selected Poems*, by Robert Hayden (Liveright). Copyright © 1975, 1972, 1970, 1966 by Robert Hayden. Reprinted by permission of Liveright Publishing Corporation.

DAVID HENDERSON: "Do Nothing till You Hear from Me" from *De Mayor of Harlem* by David Henderson (E.P. Dutton & Co.). Copyright © 1965, 1967, 1969, 1970 by David Henderson. Reprinted by permission of the publishers, E.P. Dutton, and the author.

CALVIN C. HERNTON: "Fall Down" reprinted by permission of Calvin C. Hernton.

EVERETT HOAGLAND: "The Music" from *Black World,* September 1975. Copyright © 1976 by Everett Hoagland. Reprinted by permission of *Black World,* Johnson Publishing Company, and Everett Hoagland.

LANGSTON HUGHES: "Sun Song," "Daybreak in Alabama," and "When Sue Wears Red" from *Selected Poems,* by Langston Hughes (Knopf). "Sun Song" Copyright © 1927 by Alfred A. Knopf, Inc. Renewed 1955 by Langston Hughes. "Daybreak in Alabama" copyright © 1948 by Langston Hughes. "When Sue Wears Red" copyright © 1926 by Alfred A. Knopf, Inc. Renewed 1954 by Langston Hughes. Reprinted by permission of Alfred A. Knopf, Inc. "Junior Addict," and "Lumumba's Grave" from *The Panther and the Lash: Poems of Our Times,* by Langston Hughes (Knopf). "Junior Addict" © 1963, by Langston Hughes. "Lumumba's Grave" copyright © 1967 by Arna Bontemps and George Houston Bass, executors of the estate of Langston Hughes. Reprinted by permission of the publisher and Harold Ober Associates, Inc. "Oppression" from *Fields of Wonder,* by Langston Hughes (Knopf). Copyright © 1947 by Langston Hughes. Reprinted by permission of Alfred A. Knopf, Inc.

ANGELA JACKSON: "blackmen: who make morning" first appeared in *Black World,* September 1973. Copyright © 1974 by Angela Jackson. Reprinted by permission of *Black World,* Johnson Publishing Company, and Angela Jackson.

MAE JACKSON: "i remember" from *Can I Poet with You,* by Mae Jackson. Copyright © by Mae Jackson and reprinted with her permission.

LANCE JERRERS: "Breath in My Nostrils" from *My Blackness Is the Beauty of This Land,* by Lance Jeffers (Broadside Press). Copyright © 1970 by Lance Jeffers. Reprinted by permission of Broadside Press. "Trellie," "How High the Moon," "Nina Simone," and "Who Shined Shoes in Times Square" from *When I Know the Power of My Black Hand,* by Lance Jeffers (Broadside Press). Copyright © 1974 by Lance Jeffers. Reprinted by permission of Broadside Press.

TED JOANS: "LOVE TIGHT" from *Afrodisia,* by Ted Joans (Hill & Wang). Copyright © 1970 by Ted Joans. Reprinted with the permission of Hill & Wang (now a division of Farrar, Straus & Giroux, Inc.). Permission to reprint also granted by Marion Boyars Publishers Ltd., British publishers of *Afrodisia,* by Ted Joans.

FRED JOHNSON: "Coda," and "Noises" reprinted by permission of Fred Johnson.

JOE JOHNSON: "Samurai and Hustlers," "Anna," and "True Love" copyright © 1977 by Joe Johnson and reprinted with his permission.

BOB KAUFMAN: "Unholy Missions," and "Blues Note" from *Solitudes Crowded with Loneliness,* by Bob Kaufman (New Directions). Copyright © 1965 by Bob Kaufman. Reprinted by permission of New Directions Publishing Corporation. "When We Hear the Eye Open . . ." from *Golden Sardine,* by Bob Kaufman (City Lights). Copyright © 1967 by Bob Kaufman. Reprinted by permission of City Lights Books.

ETHERIDGE KNIGHT: "The Idea of Ancestry," and "Portrait of Malcolm X" from *Poems from Prison,* by Etheridge Knight (Broadside Press). Copyright © 1968 by Etheridge Knight. Reprinted by permission of Broadside Press. "For Black Poets Who Think of Suicide" from *Black Poetry,* edited by Dudley Randall

(Broadside Press). Copyright © 1969 by Dudley Randall. Reprinted by permission of Broadside Press.

JOHARI M. KUNJUFU (formerly JOHARI M. AMINI): "(on the naming day)" from *Black World,* September, 1973. Copyright © 1973 by Johari M. Amini. Reprinted by permission of *Black World.,* Johnson Publishing Company, and Johari M. Kunjufu.

REGINALD LOCKETT: "good times & no bread" from *Black World,* December 1974. Reprinted by permission of *Black World,* Johnson Publishing Company, and Reginald Lockett.

PEARL CLEAGE LOMAX: "Jesus Drum" copyright © 1975 by Pearl Cleage Lomax. Reprinted by permission of Pearl Cleage Lomax. "Mississippi Born" copyright © 1977 by Pearl Cleage Lomax and reprinted with permission of the author. "Poem" from *We Don't Need No Music,* by Pearl Cleage Lomax (Broadside Press). Copyright © 1972 by Pearl Cleage Lomax. Reprinted by permission of Broadside Press.

DOUGHTRY LONG: "#4," "Poem No. 21," and "One Time Henry Dreamed the Number" from *Black Love, Black Hope,* by Doughtry Long (Broadside Press. Copyright © 1971 by Doughtry Long. Reprinted by permission of Broadside Press.

AUDRE LORDE: "Rites of Passage," and "Coal" from *Coal,* by Audre Lorde (W. W. Norton). Copyright © 1968, 1970, 1976 by Audre Lorde. Reprinted by permission of W. W. Norton & Company, Inc., and Hoffman-Sheedy Literary Agency. "For Each of You" from *From a Land Where Other People Live,* by Audre Lorde (Broadside Press). Copyright © 1973 by Audre Lorde Rollins. Reprinted by permission of Broadside Press. "Oya," "A Trip on the Staten Island Ferry," "One Year to Life on the Grand Central Shuttle," "A Birthday Memorial to Seventh Street," "To My Daughter the Junkie on a Train," "To Desi as Joe as Smoky the Lover of 115th Street," and "Naturally" from *New York Head Shop and Museum* by Audre Lorde. (Broadside Press). Copyright © 1974 by Audre Lorde Rollins. Reprinted by permission of Broadside Press. "Eulogy for Alvin Frost" from *Black World,* November 1975. Reprinted by permission of *Black World,* Johnson Publishing Company, and Hoffman-Sheedy Literary Agency.

K. CURTIS LYLE: "Terra Cotta" reprinted by permission of K. Curtis Lyle.

CHARLES LYNCH: "If We Cannot Live as People," and "Shade" copyright © 1977 by Charles Lynch. Reprinted by permission of Charles Lynch.

NATE MACKEY: "New and Old Gospel" from *Yardbird Reader.* Copyright © 1973 by Nate Mackey. Reprinted by permission of Nate Mackey.

HAKI R. MADHUBUTI (DON L. LEE): "from: African Poems," "Man Thinking About Woman," "change-up," and "Big momma" from *We Walk the Way of the New World,* by Haki R. Madhubuti (Don L. Lee) (Broadside Press). Copyright © 1970 by Don L. Lee. Reprinted by permission of Broadside Press.

BARBARA MAHONE: "colors for mama," and "sugarfields" from *Sugarfields,* by Barbara Mahone (privately printed, distributed by Broadside Press). Copyright © 1970 by Barbara D. Mahone. Reprinted by permission of Barbara Mahone McBain.

GLORIA ODEN: "The Way It Is" from *Poetry Is Alive and Well and Living in America,* by Gloria Oden and May Swenson (Media Plus, Inc.) Copyright © 1969 by Media Plus, Inc. and reprinted by permission of the author.

OLUMO (JIM CUNNINGHAM): "A Portrait of Rudy" from *Black World,* January

1975. Copyright © 1974 by the Johnson Publishing Company. Reprinted by permission of *Black World*, Johnson Publishing Company, and James Cunningham.

BOB O'MEALLY: "Make Music with Your Life" Copyright © 1977 by Robert O'Meally and reprinted with his permission.

LINDSAY PATTERSON: "At Long Last" from *A Rock Against the Wind*, edited by Lindsay Patterson (Dodd, Mead). Copyright © 1973 by Lindsay Patterson. Reprinted by permission of Lindsay Patterson.

RAYMOND R. PATTERSON: "Birmingham 1963" from *26 Ways of Looking at a Black Man*, by Raymond R. Patterson (Award Books). Copyright © 1969 by Raymond R. Patterson and reprinted by permission of the author.

ROB PENNY: "i remember how she sang," and "The Real People Loves One Another" copyright © 1970 by Oduduwa Productions, Inc. Reprinted by permission of Rob Penny.

FRANK LAMONT PHILLIPS: "Daybreak" from *Black World,* September 1975. Copyright © 1976 by Frank Lamont Phillips. Reprinted by permission of *Black World*, Johnson Publishing Company, and Frank Lamont Phillips.

STERLING D. PLUMPP: "For Mattie & Eternity" from *Black World*, September 1975. Reprinted by permission of *Black World*, Johnson Publishing Company, and Sterling D. Plumpp.

DUDLEY RANDALL: "Memorial Wreath," and "The Southern Road" from *Poem Counterpoem*, by Dudley Randall and Margaret Danner (Broadside Press). Copyright © 1966 by Dudley Randall and Margaret Danner. "Ancestors," and "After the Killing" from *After the Killing*, by Dudley Randall (Broadside Press). Copyright © 1973 by Dudley Randall. "Langston Blues" from *More to Remember*, by Dudley Randall (Broadside Press). Copyright 1971 © by Dudley Randall. "A Different Image," and "Roses and Revolutions" from *Cities Burning*, by Dudley Randall (Broadside Press). Copyright © 1968 by Dudley Randall. "Black Magic" from *Love You*, by Dudley Randall (Broadside Press). Copyright © 1971 by Dudley Randall. All selections reprinted with permission of Dudley Randall and Broadside Press.

EUGENE REDMOND: "Love Necessitates" from *Consider Loneliness as These Things*, by Eugene Redmond (Centro Studi E Scambi Internazionali, Italy). Copyright © 1974 by Eugene Redmond and reprinted with his permission.

ISHMAEL REED: "The Reactionary Poet" from *Hambone*. Copyright © 1973 by Ishmael Reed and reprinted by permission of the author. "Untitled I," "Instructions to a princess," and "beware: do not read this poem" from *Conjure* by Ishmael Reed (University of Massachusetts Press). Copyright © 1972 by Ishmael Reed and reprinted with his permission.

CONRAD KENT RIVERS: "Malcolm, A Thousandth Poem" from *Black World*, September 1975. Copyright © Cora McIver Rivers. Reprinted by permission of *Black World*, Johnson Publishing Company, and Cora McIver Rivers. "For All Things Black and Beautiful" from *Black World*, September 1967. Copyright © 1967 by Conrad Kent Rivers. Reprinted by permission of *Black World*, Johnson Publishing Company, and Cora McIver Rivers. "The Still Voice of Harlem" from *The Still Voice of Harlem* (Paul Bremen). Copyright © 1968 by Conrad Kent Rivers. Reprinted by permission of Cora McIver Rivers.

CAROLYN M. RODGERS: "for sapphires" copyright © 1971 by Carolyn M. Rodgers. "How i got ovah" copyright © 1973 by Carolyn M. Rodgers. "For muh' dear," "A Common Poem," and "Some Me of Beauty" copyright ©

1975 by Carolyn M. Rodgers. All selections from the book *How I Got Ovah,* by Carolyn M. Rodgers (Doubleday). Reprinted by permission of Doubleday & Company, Inc. "We Dance like Ella Riffs" from *Natural Process: An Anthology of New Black Poetry* edited by Ted Wilentz and Tom Weatherly (Hill & Wang). Copyright © 1970 by Hill & Wang, Inc. Reprinted with the permission of Hill & Wang (now a division of Farrar, Straus & Giroux, Inc.).

CHARLES ROWELL: "The Old Women Still Sing" from *Black World*, December 1974. Reprinted by permission of *Black World*, Johnson Publishing Company, and Charles H. Rowell.

SONIA SANCHEZ: "don't wanna be" from *It's a New Day* by Sonia Sanchez (Broadside Press). Copyright © 1971 by Sonia Sanchez. "Present" from *A Blues Book for Blue Black Magical Women,* by Sonia Sanchez (Broadside Press). Copyright © 1974 by Sonia Sanchez McRae. "Poem at thirty" from *Homecoming,* by Sonia Sanchez (Broadside Press). Copyright © 1969 by Sonia Sanchez. "Now poem.   for us." from *We a Baddddd People,* by Sonia Sanchez (Broadside Press). Copyright © 1970 by Sonia Sanchez Knight. All selections reprinted by permission of Broadside Press.

JUDY DOTHARD SIMMONS: "Alabama" copyright © 1972 by Judy Dothard Simmons. "Survivor," and "it's comforting" copyright © 1977 by Judy Dothard Simmons. All reprinted by permission of Judy D. Simmons. "Generations" from *Judith's Blues,* by Judy Dothard Simmons (Broadside Press). Copyright © 1973 by Judy Dothard Simmons. Reprinted by permission of Broadside Press.

A. B. SPELLMAN: "For My Unborn & Wretched Children," "John coltrane an impartial review," "tomorrow the heroes," and "when black people are" reprinted by permission of A. B. Spellman.

JOYCE CAROL THOMAS: "Poem for Otis Redding," "The M J Q," and "Church Poem" copyright © 1973 by Joyce Carol Thomas. "I Know A Lady," and "Where is the Black Community?" copyright © 1974 by Joyce Carol Thomas. All selections reprinted by permission of Joyce Carol Thomas.

QUINCY TROUPE: "Transformation," "For Malcolm Who Walks in the Eyes of Our Children," and "The Old People Speak of Death" from *Ash Doors and Juju Guitars,* by Quincy Troupe (Random House). Copyright © 1973, 1977, by Quincy Troupe. "South African Bloodstone" from *Embryo,* by Quincy Troupe (Barlenmir House). Copyright © 1972 by Quincy Troupe. All selections reprinted by permission of Quincy Troupe.

MARGARET WALKER: "Lineage," and "For My People" from *For My People* by Margaret Walker (Yale University Press). Copyright © 1942, 1970, 1977 by Margaret Walker and reprinted with her permission. "For Malcolm X," "Street Demonstration," and "Girl Held Without Bail" from *Prophets for a New Day,* by Margaret Walker (Broadside Press). Copyright © 1970 by Margaret Walker Alexander. Reprinted by permission of Broadside Press.

RON WELBURN: "Percussions" copyright © 1977 by Ron Welburn, and reprinted with his permission.

AL YOUNG: "Myself When I Am Real" from *Dancing* (Corinth). Copyright © 1969 by Al Young. Reprinted by permission of Al Young and Ted Wilentz. "For Poets" copyright © 1968 by Al Young and reprinted by permission of the author. "The Song Turning Back into Itself" copyright © 1968, 1969, and 1971 by Al Young and reprinted by permission of the author.

YVONNE: "Where She Was Not Born," "Emma," and "Deborah Lee" copyright © 1974, 1976 by Yvonne and reprinted by permission of the author.

Thanks

Marci Carafoli, poet, editor, and friend, for her vision, work, and dedication. Hundreds of poets and teachers like Quincy Troupe, Hoyt Fuller, Dudley Randall, Yvonne, and many others, for all their help in finding materials and poets. Many librarians in New York City; Yellow Springs, Ohio; and in cities around the country, who helped in the search and research. My family, Virginia Hamilton Adoff, and Leigh and Jaime Adoff, for their love and patience in living with piles of paper and my ragged nerves over the past years.

Index

Authors' names are printed in capitals, titles of poems in italics, and first lines of poems in ordinary roman type.